THE WORD IN WORSHIP

Abingdon Preacher's Library

THE WORD IN WORSHIP
Preaching in a Liturgical Context

William Skudlarek

ABINGDON PREACHER'S LIBRARY

William D. Thompson, Editor

ABINGDON
Nashville

The Word in Worship: Preaching in a Liturgical Context

Copyright © 1981 by Abingdon

Library of Congress Cataloging in Publication Data

SKUDLAREK, WILLIAM.
  The word in worship.
  (Abingdon preacher's library)
  Bibliography: p.
  Includes index.
  1. Preaching. 2. Liturgics. 3. Lectionaries. I. Title.
  BV4211.2.S538   264'.6   80-25525

ISBN 0-687-46131-6 (pbk.)

Scripture quotations are from the Revised Standard Version Common Bible,
copyright © 1973 by the Division of Christian Education of the National Council of
the Churches of Christ in the U.S.A., and are used by permission.

MANUFACTURED BY THE PARTHENON PRESS AT
NASHVILLE, TENNESSEE, UNITED STATES OF AMERICA

CONTENTS

EDITOR'S FOREWORD

Preaching has captured the attention of increasingly large segments of the American public. Lay parish committees seeking pastoral leadership consistently rank preaching as the most desirable pastoral skill. Seminary courses and clergy conferences on preaching attract participants in larger numbers than ever. Millions of viewers watch television preachers every week.

What is *good* preaching? is the question of both those who hear it and those who do it. Hearers answer that question instinctively, tuning in the preacher who meets their needs, whether in the pulpit of the neighborhood church or on a broadcast. Preachers need to answer more intentionally.

Time was that a good thick book on preaching would do it, or a miscellaneous smattering of thin ones. The time now seems ripe for a different kind of resource—a carefully conceived, tightly edited series of books whose scope covers the homiletical spectrum and whose individual volumes reveal the latest and best thinking about each specialty within the field of preaching. The volumes in the Abingdon Preacher's Library enable the preacher to understand preaching in its historical setting; to examine its biblical and theological underpinnings; to explore its spiritual, relational, and liturgical dimensions; and to develop insights into its craftsmanship.

Designed primarily for use in the seminary classroom, this series will also serve the practicing preacher whose background in homiletics is spotty or out-of-date, or whose preaching needs strengthening in some specific area.

William D. Thompson
Eastern Baptist Theological Seminary
Philadelphia, Pennsylvania

PREFACE

Preaching at its finest is preaching that is biblically centered, directed to the real questions of people, and taken up in worship. The past generation of Roman Catholics and Protestants experienced, for the most part, a form of worship that was a mere torso—a sacramental service without preaching, a preaching service without the sacrament. Today that regrettable maiming of our worship is being healed. While there is no denying that both Catholics and Protestants are still a long way from achieving a pattern of worship that is the vibrant expression of praise and thanksgiving by a people who, because of the inspired preaching of their pastors and teachers, are able to discern the word of God in their lives, we can be grateful that the church today seems well on the way to redressing the distortion of its worship that had been centuries in the making. This book is offered to all those men and women in the church who hear the call to preach the good news in order that people may be led to faith, and from faith to praise and thanksgiving.

The writing of this book would not have been possible without the "help of many brethren," which the Benedictine Rule puts forth as an essential element of monastic community life. It gives me special pleasure in this, the fifteen-hundredth anniversary of St. Benedict's birth, to thank not only my brothers at Collegeville, who are a constant source of support for me, but also Abbot Raphael De Salvo and the monks of Subiaco Abbey in Arkansas, who graciously took me into their community for a time and afforded me the facilities and leisure I needed to bring this work to completion. To all of them, and in a special way to Jerome Kodell, O.S.B., and Victor Klimoski, I express my deep appreciation for helpful suggestions and encouraging support.

I. THE BIBLE
AND THE LITURGICAL YEAR

Christians have come to take the liturgical context of preaching for granted. Even though we may speak of churches that are nonliturgical, we find that when their members gather for worship, they do so for a service that includes more than just a sermon. Normally we find various forms of prayer (common recitation, prayer offered by one in the name of all, spontaneous outbursts), music and song, public reading, common posture and gestures. All this is liturgy, the work of the people.[1]

What varies from church to church, of course, is the form this liturgy takes. In some churches the emphasis is on movement, color, scent, and sound. In others there is a determined effort to keep everything as lean and simple as possible. Some churches highlight the sermon; others the vocal participation of the community in prayer and song. Some congregations stress order and uniformity in their gatherings; others allow much freer reign to individual expression and the movement of the Spirit. But these services are all liturgical to the degree that they are conceived and celebrated as a communal act of worship. Some ecclesial traditions give greater attention to a formal definition of what makes a particular act of worship an official act of the church rather than simply an act of individuals within it. But such a legalistic concern with the official nature of liturgy must always remain secondary to concern for its communal and participatory nature.

In these varied expressions of Christian liturgy, however, there is one element that is common to all, and that is the presence of the scriptures. No matter how formal or informal, how solemn or simple, how large or small the gathering may be, the scriptures are present, either by means of a formal reading of the text or by way of quotation or allusion in the prayers and hymns. Christian (and Jewish) worship flows out of a word of remembrance that has come down to us in a text. When we assemble in worship we do so in response to a word that calls and gathers us; and the very words by which we give expression to our longing, our sorrow, our praise and thanksgiving, are inspired by the words that we have received.

The centrality of the word in Christian worship is also to be seen in the fact that this word is not only read from a book but is interpreted and applied to the life of the worshiping community through that form of oral communication we call preaching. The text of scripture comes to expression[2] in preaching in order that it may more easily be heard as the word of God, promising salvation to his people, inviting them to hear that word in faith, and thus enabling them to respond in praise and thanksgiving.

Because the word of scripture is the indispensable foundation not only of preaching but of the church's life of worship, any study of liturgical preaching must begin with a consideration of the way scripture is used in the church's worship. How, out of the wealth of teaching, story, and prayer that we find in the Bible, do Christian preachers and communities choose what to read and hear on a particular day when they gather for worship?

FREE SELECTION OF TEXTS

It is, of course, possible to reject any system and simply to choose a passage from the Bible at random and make that the basis of the sermon. Although it is conceivable that preachers who approach the scriptures in this way might try to justify their practice with an appeal to Paul's gospel of Christian freedom or the text from the Gospel of John that speaks about the Spirit blowing where it will (3:8), it should be obvious that such total absence of order or plan is in no way conducive to intelligent preaching or intelligent hearing. Contemporary New Testament scholarship makes it abundantly clear that the arrangement of material in each of the Gospels is ordered according to the particular Evangelist's theological purpose or intention. The authors did not simply string stories together in a haphazard fashion. They ordered them in a certain way because of the point they wanted to make. The Evangelists' concern for order and purpose in the presentation of the Gospel belongs to the preacher as well.

Approaching the choice of the scripture to be read and expounded with an attitude of total and absolute freedom is probably not very common with preachers. But what is common is the choosing of those texts which the preacher for personal reasons finds appealing or suitable for preaching. Such a method of choosing texts soon gives congregations the impression that they are simply at the whim of the preacher's fancy. An eloquent statement of the laity's resentment of this practice is to be found in a letter from a blacksmith to the ministers and elders of the Church of Scotland, written in 1758:

> It is true you indulge us now and then with ten or a dozen of verses of pure scripture in our publick assemblies, but as we have no regular plan of reading the scriptures, of consequence we only hear detached places, chosen at the pleasure of the preacher, and applied to what purposes he thinks fit; this leaves our understanding too much in the power of the clergy, and exposes the simple and the ignorant . . . to be seduced by the party principles and whimsical opinions of the preachers. It may at first sight appear, that the whole plan of our worship, is as happily calculated for making a property of the laity, and keeping their judgments and consciences in the power of the person, as any part of the popish system; for the minister needs not read any part of the scriptures unless he pleases; he may choose what place he thinks proper, may begin where he inclines, and break off when he has a mind; he may mangle them in any manner he think fit, and make them say whatever he would have them say.[3]

It need hardly be added that while the free selection of passages from the scriptures is not calculated to produce resentment on the part of the laity, it will contribute just as surely to the laziness and narrowness of the clergy who will often be tempted to return to their favorite texts and to reach into their sermon files for a "once more with feeling" delivery of something they put together in their younger and more energetic days.

A third way of approaching the Bible freely for the selection of texts for preaching is one that might be termed the pastoral approach.

Here the preacher selects from the Bible a passage that seems to provide a response to a human situation, either particular or general, which the sermon will address. This method has obvious advantages and a good deal of attraction. It is, as may be obvious to many readers, the life-situation approach to preaching, whose greatest apologist and practitioner on the American scene may well have been Harry Emerson Fosdick. Preaching of this kind is concerned to address people "where they're at" and demands that the sermon not simply make a point but solve a problem. When competently done, it ensures that preaching not drift off into heady abstractions but remain in touch with the lives of real people.

For a good number of contemporary preachers it is unacceptable that "the preacher should be a passive participant in the preaching event's most significant decision."[4] And this is precisely the case, so it is said, when the pastoral principle is abandoned and the preacher permits the lectionary to choose the scriptural text for the sermon.

The reason this pastoral principle is so strongly defended by many preachers is that they insist, and rightly so, that it is for the preacher to decide what the word of God is for this people, this week. As will, I hope, become clear in what follows, I agree entirely with this position. My contention, however, is that such a determination can be made, in fact is more creatively and engagingly made, on the basis of an ordered reading of the scriptures, with which a lectionary provides us.

Although the choice of texts on the basis of pastorally perceived need can make for preaching that is immediate and powerful, it is not without its own problems. The first of these is that a preacher who picks a text because it can help direct the word of God to a particular problem or situation indicates that one already knows in advance what the word of God is going to be. We pick this text rather than that text because we are sure that this is what God is saying to these people at this time. Of course, there is always the possibility that serious exegetical study and prayer may show us that our choice was not necessarily a good one, but once we have made the choice it is far more likely that we will (unconsciously, of course!) do our studying and praying in such a way as to convince ourselves of the accuracy and appropriateness of our selection.

A more basic difficulty with this approach to the choice of texts for preaching is that it tends to make the hearer the source rather than the recipient of preaching. Scripture is seen as an answer book, even to questions that its authors never had to face. However, if scripture provides answers (and it does), these answers are given to questions that, more often than not, the scriptures have themselves provoked. These questions concern the ultimate meaning of our existence rather than the penultimate and antepenultimate concern of our everyday lives. As Jean-Jacques von Allmen puts it, "The truth is that we cannot ask the real existential questions until we have been brought face to face with the Word of God."[5] In a similar vein Gustaf Wingren writes: "[The Bible] claims the right to formulate these questions itself. The Word loses part of its content when it is made to reply to questions other than those that spring from the Word itself."[6]

SYSTEMATIC READING OF SCRIPTURE

The most obvious way of engaging in a systematic reading of scripture would be to take a book of the Bible and read it from cover to cover. This practice of a continuous reading of scripture (*lectio continua*, as it is technically called) is rooted in Jewish and Christian antiquity and was strongly promoted by major figures in the sixteenth-century Protestant Reformation (especially Calvin and Zwingli) as an alternative to the "bits and pieces" approach to the Bible that they found in the Roman Catholic mass of the time. One can occasionally find this method of reading and preaching promoted at the present time. J. Winston Pearce, for example, devotes a chapter in his book on sermon planning to "Preaching Through the Bible." "The idea," he writes," "is to begin in Genesis and move straight through to Revelation, no matter how long the journey may take."[7]

When we come to study the composition of the liturgical lectionaries currently in use in many Christian denominations, we will see that a modified *lectio continua of the scriptures is employed in them. In itself, however, the lectio continua* principle has no relation to the cycle of feasts and seasons that makes up the Christian year. In fact, its adoption by some of the more insistent Protestant movements was a way of protesting against the observance of festivals, new moons, and sabbaths, which are "only a shadow of what is to come" (Col. 2:17). If one were to adopt this manner of reading and preaching from scripture, it would be just as appropriate to read Isaiah in June as in December, or the Acts of the Apostles during Lent as during the Easter season.

Even apart from the consideration of the appropriate time to read certain sections of the Bible, it seems to me that to appeal to the principle of *lectio continua* in an absolute way is at odds with the goal of effective preaching from the scriptures. To read a book through from beginning to end may be a helpful way of teaching scripture, but not necessarily of preaching it. If the preacher is too concerned to deal with "the book," to treat such questions as its origin, author, setting, and genre, the sermon can all too easily turn into a lecture on a particular book or passage of the Bible, rather than a preached word that uses the scriptural word to bring the word of God to expression here and now. The *lectio continua* of the scriptures certainly allows for such contact with the lives and concerns of the hearers, but it opens the possibility that this concern will become secondary, if present at all, to a narrow preoccupation with the text. And while there may never have been a preacher who approached the pulpit convinced that "folks come to church desperately anxious to discover what happened to the Jebusites,"[8] Fosdick's critique of the distortion of preaching which results from a one-sided concern with the text is well made and still valid.

Finally, before turning to a consideration of the liturgical lectionary as a method of reading and preaching from scripture, we might consider the possibility of an arrangement of scriptural reading worked out according to principles other than the church year.

The organization of scriptural lessons around points of doctrine or ethics is certainly a possibility. The problem with such an approach to the scriptures, however, is that it tends to make the liturgical worship of the Christian community primarily an occasion for a program of Christian education. This is not to deny that there is a great need in the church for ongoing catechesis. Nor can one deny that apart from the Sunday morning service it is very difficult to reach more than a small minority of the community in any sustained way. But the solution to these problems is not to turn the church into a classroom. We will come out ahead in the long run, I believe, if we approach the time of worship as a time to celebrate the God who is present and active in people's lives, and design programs of Christian education that flow out of the liturgical experience and offer people the opportunity to reflect on the meaning of this present and active God. A reading and study of the scriptures organized according to some doctrinal or ethical outline would, I believe, be appropriate for such gatherings. In the liturgical assembly a pattern of scriptural reading centered on the person and mysteries of Christ, that is, a pattern organized around the Christian year, is much to be preferred.

THE JEWISH ORIGINS OF THE LECTIONARY

The liturgical lectionary has a long history, reaching back into the pre-Christian origins of our traditions of worship. The public reading of sacred writings was certainly common in ancient Jewish ritual, although to say, as Eric Warner does, that "it seems probable that the public reading of sacred writings was once a unique feature of ancient Jewish ritual"[9] may need modification in the light of our knowledge of the religious practices of other ancient Near Eastern peoples. For example, we know that at Babylon the recitation of the creation story (Eneuma Elish) had to take place during the late afternoon of the fourth day of the new year celebration.[10]

In Jewish tradition the orderly reading of the scriptures was a special feature of the synagogue services and was looked upon as a substitute for the sacrifice that was the monopoly of the central sanctuary. In this synagogue service the practice developed of reading two lessons. The first of these consisted of a reading from the Torah (Pentateuch), which in the so-called Palestinian cycle was divided into 150 portions (called *seder* or *parashah*) and spread out over three years. In the so-called Babylonian cycle the entire Pentateuch was read in the course of one year. There may also have been a three-year cycle of psalm readings, and this practice may account for the inclusion of a reference to the Book of Psalms in the words of Jesus recorded in the Gospel of Luke: "Everything written about me in the law of Moses, and the prophets and the psalms must be fulfilled" (24:44).[11]

The second lesson, called the *haftara* (dismissal) because it was read at the end of the service, was taken from the prophetic books. This lesson was not a *lectio continua* of the prophets. Rather, it was chosen to correspond to the section of the Torah that had been read, or to provide the scriptural basis for some of the holy days of the Jewish year. A reference to this use of prophetic texts in the synagogue service may perhaps be found in the Lucan account of Jesus in the synagogue at Nazareth (4:16-30). Luke writes that Jesus "found" the passage in Isaiah. According to some exegetes, this indicates that the prophetic portion "had previously been prepared and marked in the scroll by the archisynagogus or another official in such a way that Jesus could easily find the prescribed passage."[12] Jesus, in other words, was reading and preaching from the *haftara* assigned for that particular day.

If we may be permitted to anticipate our discussion of the revised Christian lectionaries in use in the church today, we can at this point note the striking similarity between the principles that guided the formation of the Palestinian cycle of the Jewish lectionary and those which were followed by the originators of current lectionaries. Their main feature is a continuous reading of each of the three Synoptic Gospels. On each Sunday a reading from the Old Testament is selected to parallel the gospel lesson that is to be read on that day. Thus, the gospel, the new law, is treated like the Torah, and the Old Testament reading like the prophetic *haftara*.

We might also note in passing that some contemporary New Testament scholars are working with the hypothesis that a lectionary framework is to be found in the very composition of the Gospels. Most of the work to date has been done on the Gospels of Mark and John. If the lectionary hypothesis can be proven—although there are those who doubt that it can—it would reinforce the commonly accepted position that the Gospels are not chronological records of the words and deeds of

Jesus. Instead the Gospel may be a series of liturgical lessons adapted to the already existing lessons of the synagogue cycle. The one-year ministry of Jesus in the Gospel of Mark, for example, would be explained by the fact that the author was working with a lectionary based on the calendar year.[13]

Although it seems clear that the practice of the synagogue was influential in promoting the development of lectionaries for use in Christian worship, we find little evidence for such arrangements of scripture for use in worship before the third century. And when lectionaries do begin to make their appearance (or, if not lectionaries, then at least evidence for the practice of reading certain parts of the Bible at certain times of the year: Acts before Pentecost, Acts and Revelation between Easter and Pentecost, Genesis during Lent, Job and John in Passion Week), that appearance was due to the development of the liturgical year. However, since the Christian observance of time emerged from the weekly celebration of the Lord's resurrection, we must first of all consider the influence of Sunday on the development of the church's liturgy.

THE LORD'S DAY AND THE EUCHARIST

It was the week rather than the year that constituted the primary unit of time for the first Christians. The resurrection of Christ had changed everything for his followers. His mission had been vindicated; his defeat was not final; he was alive and with them. The profound impact that the resurrection had on them can be seen in the fact that they began a regular practice of gathering for worship on the day of the week on which he rose and on which he sent his Holy Spirit. New Testament references to the special significance of the first day of the week for the early Christian community are to be found in Acts 20:7-11 and Revelation 1:10. In Acts, Luke recounts the somewhat too lengthy discourse (at least for Eutychus!) Paul gave to the community at Troas on the "first day of the week, when we were gathered to break bread." And in Revelation, John refers to his vision on Patmos, which took place on "the Lord's Day" (*kyriake hemera* rather than *hemera Kyriou*, the latter "day of the Lord" referring to the Lord's coming in judgment at the end of time).

From all the evidence we have, this observance of the Lord's day was explicitly tied to the resurrection of Christ. It was a Christian creation, and was not thought of as substituting for or, for that matter, prolonging the Jewish Sabbath. The Lord's Day was not a day of rest for the early Christians. That was still the Sabbath, which, it seems, they continued to observe, even attending the synagogue.[14] But on the first day of the week they would gather for the apostles' teaching, the breaking of the bread, and for prayers (see Acts 2:42).[15]

According to an interpretation of liturgical history that has gained a good deal of acceptance, especially in the way it was proposed by Dom Gregory Dix in his classic work, *The Shape of the Liturgy*,[16] early Christian worship was originally composed of two separate elements: the synaxis (or gathering), modeled on the service of reading, commentary, and prayer that originated in the synagogue; and the table service or breaking of the bread, which was peculiarly Christian in its origin and significance. According to the proponents of this theory, the first solid evidence we have for the joining of the two elements is the description of the Sunday assembly of Christians in Rome given by Justin Martyr in his first Apology, written around 150:

> On the day which is called Sunday we have a common assembly of all who live in the cities or in the outlying districts, and the memoirs of the Apostles or the writings of the Prophets are read, as long as there is time. Then, when the reader has finished, the president of the assembly verbally admonishes and invites all to imitate such examples of virtue. Then we all stand up together and offer up our prayers, and, as we said before, after we finish our prayers, bread and wine and water are presented. He who presides likewise offers up prayers and thanksgivings, to the best of his ability, and the people express their approval by saying "Amen." The Eucharistic elements are distributed and consumed by those present, and to those who are absent they are sent through the deacons. The wealthy, if they wish, contribute whatever they desire, and the collection is placed in the custody of the president. [With it] he helps the orphans and widows, those who are needy because of sickness or any other reason, and the captives and strangers in our midst; in short, he takes

care of all those in need. Sunday, indeed, is the day on which we all hold our common assembly because it is the first day on which God, transforming the darkness and [prime] matter, created the world; and our Savior Jesus Christ arose from the dead on the same day. For they crucified Him on the day before that of Saturn, and on the day after, which is Sunday, He appeared to His Apostles and disciples, and taught them the things which we have passed on to you also for consideration.[17]

It may well be true that this remarkable passage from the middle of the second century provides us with the first solid evidence we have for the joining together of what has come to be called, in the Roman rite, the liturgy of the word and the liturgy of the eucharist. Nonetheless, it seems to me that one could construct a rather strong argument for the hypothesis that while there may have been liturgies of the word without eucharist (that is, a gathering for the hearing of the scriptures and for prayer, modeled on the synagogue service), there was no eucharist without a liturgy of the word. The most compelling argument for this hypothesis, I believe, is the fact that the Christian "breaking of bread" was done in memory of the meals that Jesus took with his followers, and preeminently of the meal that he took with them "on the night when he was betrayed" and in which he "took bread, and when he had given thanks, he broke it, and said, 'This is my body which is for you. Do this in remembrance of me' " (I Cor. 11:23-24).

This last supper of Jesus with his disciples is described by the Evangelists as a Passover meal. In this meal the prayers of thanksgiving (the *berakoth*) were invariably preceded by the *haggada*, the recital of the great saving acts of God for his people during the Exodus. It was the duty of the leader of the feast to recall these events so that the participants could give thanks for what God had done for them. They were to remember what God had accomplished in the past and was still accomplishing, and out of this memorial turn to God with prayers of blessing over the elements that made up the meal.

Jesus' words "Do this in remembrance of me" are directly related to the function of the *haggada* preceding the *berakoth* in the Passover meal. When his followers gather for a religious meal (in Jewish piety, the adjective is almost redundant) and remember the great and mighty acts of God, they are to remember *him* in whom God accomplished the greatest and mightiest of his deeds. He is to be the preeminent motive for the prayers of praise and thanksgiving. Through the passion and death of Jesus, the Father has shown the infinite immensity of his love for his people. In his resurrection he has shown his power over the forces of sin and death. In his exaltation in glory he offers the hope of victory to all who follow him. It is by remembering these things that the faithful followers of Jesus find themselves called to respond with a prayer of blessing. They are enabled to make eucharist.

It is difficult to imagine how the followers of Jesus, even from earliest times, could have come together for the breaking of bread without recalling him in whose name they were gathered. And this remembering, this *anamnesis* as it is technically called, is really what the liturgy of the word is all about. The words and deeds of Jesus would be recalled by means of the oral tradition that was circulating among his followers, or, at a later date, by means of the written traditions that gradually were gathered and edited into the Gospels. We find already in the writings of Paul an awareness that certain words came "from the Lord" (see I Cor. 7:12, 15), and he very likely made use of such words when he "talked on and on" to the gathered community at Troas before breaking bread with them.

We can also see in the description of the meal that the risen Lord took with the disciples at Emmaus an indication of the fact that the breaking of bread was preceded by a "liturgy of the word." The meal in the house at which "he took the bread and blessed, and broke it, and gave it to them" was preceded by his conversation en route during which "beginning with Moses and all the prophets, he interpreted to them in all the scriptures the things concerning himself" (Luke 24:30, 27). Not only does this passage indicate the pattern of Christian eucharist (taking, blessing, breaking, distributing, all done in response to the word of God), but it may also indicate that the liturgy of the word for these early Christians was composed in large part of the christological reading of the Torah, the prophets, and the psalms, as can be seen from the words of Jesus to his followers, which Luke records later in the same chapter: "These are my words which I spoke to you, while I was still with you, that everything written about me in the law of Moses and the prophets and the psalms must be fulfilled" (24:44).

As will be clear to those who have some knowledge of the origins of Christian worship, this brief treatment of the relation between the ritual of word and gesture in Christian eucharist has not taken up the problem of the dissociation of the Christian eucharist from its setting in an actual meal. This meal setting is absent in the Sunday eucharistic service of the Roman Christians around 150 that we saw described in the Apology of Justin. But only a few decades earlier, according to the description and prayers given in another early Christian document known as the *Didache*, or *Teaching of the Twelve Apostles*,[18] the eucharist is obviously celebrated in the context of a meal, with a blessing over the cup, the prayer of blessing for the breaking of bread, and then, after the meal, a long grace over the cup of blessing. Sometimes between the time of the *Didache* and the time of Justin, the most profound change in the external rite of the eucharist took place. "Somehow," writes Leonel Mitchell, "the Lord's supper was separated from the meal and acquired the format with which we are familiar: that of a service of worship. What happened is clear, but we do not know exactly when, where, or why the change was made."[19]

But, even though this change did profoundly affect the way in which the eucharist was celebrated, and without doubt profoundly altered the way it was understood and experienced, I believe my point can still stand: the observance of the eucharist is accompanied (most fittingly preceded) by a service of the word in which the community remembers the one in whose death and resurrection the new and eternal covenant came into being. It is within this pattern of word and eucharist, which is central to the church's observance of the Lord's day, that preaching can find its fullest and richest expression. With the word of God as source and motive, the preacher/presider invites a particular gathered community to model its life on "all the beautiful things it has heard," to give a literal rendering of Justin's description of the address of the president of the eucharistic assembly.[20] Having done this, prayers and thanksgivings are then offered up and the people express their approval by saying "Amen."

THE LITURGICAL YEAR

While the weekly eucharistic celebration of the Lord's resurrection continued to be observed by Christians, and eventually took to itself the rest motif of the Sabbath, a yearly commemoration of the Lord's resurrection, and subsequently of the other mysteries of his life, gradually came to be observed. In order to understand the origins of this observance, we need look no farther than the common experience of people who take note of and mark by special observances the regular return of times and seasons that indicate the passing of years. To remember what happened a year ago, to mark the turning of a year *(anni versio)*, is a natural and almost spontaneous gesture for us. By so doing we identify ourselves with our histories and we reaffirm our present identities, which are rooted in those histories.

And so it must have been for the first Christians. While they gathered every Sunday to celebrate the resurrection of their Lord, it is virtually impossible to believe that there would not have been a special intensity to the gathering that took place at that time of the year when the Passover was celebrated, the commemoration of the delivery from slavery in Egypt, which gradually came to be seen not as the last and mightiest of God's works but as a prefiguration of the Passover made by Jesus to the Father in which all his followers had been called to share. The fact that the actual death and resurrection of Jesus had been so closely identified with the annual observance of the Jewish Passover, not only in terms of chronological coincidence, but in its deepest interpretation, means that an annual observance of the resurrection, understood as an intensification of the weekly celebration, would be natural as well as religiously significant.

Once the annual celebration of Easter began to be observed, it began to radiate forward to Pentecost and backward to Holy Week and Lent. The development of these seasons is a complicated one and scholarly disagreement over some of the issues involved need not detain us here.[21] Two observations, however, are particularly important and noteworthy. The first is that while the development of the Holy Week and Easter cycles took place largely in fourth-century Jerusalem and was closely related to liturgical observances at the different holy places in that city, the liturgy never turned into mere historical reminiscing or play acting. There was a realization, whether conscious or not, that what was central to the liturgical celebration of the mystery of Christ was not some dramatic reenactment of a particular phase of the life of Jesus, but rather, in the words of Louis Bouyer, "our actual participation in the one and complete action already accomplished by Jesus, made present by our participating in His risen life, for the purpose of bringing to fruition in us all the virtualities of the final and perfect kingdom of God."[22] Bouyer goes on to argue that there was little concern for verisimilitude in the celebration of Holy Thursday, Good Friday, or Easter Sunday in Jerusalem. The account of Egeria, a Spanish nun who made a pilgrimage to the Holy Land around the year 400, he says, shows that the whole passion was read on the Mount of Olives on Easter Sunday. Actually, the reference to the reading of the passion is in connection with her description of a regular Sunday office.[23] The fifth-century Armenian Lectionary, however, does refer to the reading of the entire passion on Easter day. It is always the whole mystery of Christ's death-resurrection-glorification that is celebrated in the liturgy, even though a particular liturgical celebration may isolate one or the other event from Christ's life for special emphasis.

The second observation to be made on the development of the Lenten-Easter cycle is that the season of Lent is directly related to the preparation of the catechumens for baptism and not to an extended meditation on the sufferings of Christ. At the beginning of Lent those catechumens who were judged ready for baptism at Easter were elected by the community to begin the final phase of their preparation, a period of intense prayer and catechesis. In this catechesis we again see emphasis on the totality of the mystery of Christ. For example, Cyril of Jerusalem (bishop *ca*. 350–387) structures his catechetical lectures on the framework of the Apostles' Creed.

Both of these observations, it seems to me, have significant consequences for liturgical preaching. Such preaching is not directly concerned with Bible history, with the sequence of events, with the description of the way things were back then. Its concern, rather, is with the way in which the followers of Christ currently share in the mystery of God's life in the world, as this was preeminently revealed in the life, death, and resurrection of Jesus. Even more precisely, liturgical preaching speaks to the ways in which those who are being called to or who already share in God's life through baptism into Christ, can manifest that life in their lives. The preacher who takes the liturgical year seriously uses it to focus on now one, now another element of the mystery of Christ, but always with the concern to preach the whole Christ, Christ glorified, active, and present in his church. The calendar is seen "not as a collection of special days, but as a Christ-centered whole, repeatedly reminding us of events in the saving work of Christ."[24] The year itself is utilized as the great and permanent proclamation by the church of the word with which it has been entrusted.

Following the development of the Easter cycle, and radiating outward from it, the Christmas-Epiphany cycle came into being. Although play-acting and sentimentality (to say nothing of pure and simple commercialism) dominate many contemporary observances of this season, the concerns that lay at its origin were christological and pastoral. The Christmas cycle developed as a forceful statement of the church's belief in the divine nature of Christ, and as a way of counteracting the pagan celebrations of *sol invictus* (the unconquered sun). Needless to say, preachers today still need to wrestle with ways of expressing in forceful contemporary language the church's faith that Jesus is the Son of God, and to offer him to our world as an alternative to, indeed, at times even a rejection of, the values of this world.

As can be seen from even this cursory description of the development of the liturgical year, its predominant characteristic is christological. It is Christ, the risen Christ, who came into this world in the humble surroundings of Bethlehem, died on a cross, was raised, and is now seated at the right hand of the Father, who is at the center of this year. While the year does not exist to provide us with a dramatic reenactment of the significant events of his earthly life, it is rooted in time and history because time and history were so profoundly tied up with the interpretation of his death and resurrection. He was baptized "in the fifteenth year of the reign of Tiberius Caesar" (Luke 3:1), crucified on the preparation day for the Passover (John 19:14). According to John, he was sentenced to death at noon, the period when the priests began to slaughter Passover lambs in the temple.[25] His resurrection takes place on the third day, and, in the Lucan account, his final appearance and ascension on the fortieth day.

Thus, the reason that the liturgical year is so centered on Christ, and more specifically on his death, resurrection, and glorification, is that the love and mercy of God were revealed in the historical figure, Jesus of Nazareth. To follow the liturgical year becomes a way of affirming the concrete historical reality of this revelation.[26] At the same time, to observe this year not as a mere sequential remembering of the major events in Christ's life, but as a celebration of the total Passover mystery, prevents the observance from becoming an empty charade.

DIFFICULTIES WITH THE LITURGICAL YEAR

One of the weaknesses of the liturgical year, at least according to some commentators, is that the christological emphasis makes it, in fact, a half year, extending from Christmas (with Advent as a preparatory season) to Pentecost.[27] The period known as the season after Pentecost or Trinity ("Ordinary Time" in the Roman Catholic calendar) is not marked by any special connection with events in the life of Christ. Until the appearance of the new lectionaries, it was simply filled in with scriptural lessons that lacked both unity and continuity.

One response to this situation was to propose a lectionary in which the traditional Christian half year would be developed into a "complete liturgical cycle, manifesting the whole sweep of the Christian Religion according to the order of the Credo."[28] Another solution was the introduction of Kingdomtide, beginning on the last Sunday of August and running to Advent, a season centered on the kingdom of Christ "as it challenges men in their daily lives and every area of their existence."[29]

As logical and modest as these proposals appear, it seems to me that they err in trying to impose a theological or ethical framework on the year. The year is not a convenient way to organize the whole of Christian faith so that we may, year by year, review the essential teachings of the church. Even less, I believe, should it be an occasion for the regular consideration of certain doctrinal or ethical themes, as has at times been suggested. It is the orderly celebration of the mystery of Christ, come to fullest expression in the Paschal mystery of his death and resurrection. It is for this reason that the decision of the lectionary commission of the Second Vatican Council to organize the half year from Pentecost to Advent around the Gospels of Matthew, Mark, and Luke, rather than around any doctrinal or ethical systems, strikes me as a solution of genius. To organize the year around a Gospel makes it clear that the whole year is centered on Christ. From Advent to Pentecost we concentrate on the mysteries of his life and death. During the remainder of the year we continue our celebration of Christ, with our view guided by one of the Gospel portraits that have been given to us. Preaching, then, can be seen for what it is: not the presentation of the systematic theological teaching of the church, but the proclamation of Christ for this time and place, upon which and out of which the church's systematic reflection takes place.

One of the frequently voiced concerns about the difficulty of observing the liturgical year is that one finds oneself so frequently in conflict with secular holidays. However, I think the problem is not so much one of conflict with the secular calendar, as it is of the conflict with all those special Sundays (Education Sunday, World Mission Sunday, Vocation Sunday, Universal Day of Prayer for Students) that tend to fill up denominational calendars. As we become more aware that the purpose of the liturgical year, and of the liturgy generally, is to celebrate our share in the mystery of Christ and not to take advantage of peoples' coming together in order to indoctrinate them or organize them for some special project, such thematic designations of various Sundays throughout the year should diminish. To the extent that they remain in denominational calendars, they may be discreetly observed by preachers and pastors with a note in the church bulletin or a petition in the intercessory prayers. They certainly need not determine the shape of the liturgy or the content of the preaching.

As for those other times when widely observed secular holidays (for example, Mother's Day or the Fourth of July) come along, it will do no good to say that the preachers should simply ignore them as having nothing to do with Christian worship. The fact is that everyone is aware of what day it is, and attempts on the part of the preacher to ignore a particular holiday will only call attention to it in a way that will either damage the preacher's credibility or evoke resistance to the message that is offered.

But, on the other hand, the solution is not to ignore the church calendar or to adjust it in such a way that the secular holiday becomes the center of the church's celebration. If the celebration of Pentecost is delayed a week or simply omitted so that Mother's Day can be observed, a Christian community may be indicating in a rather striking way that motherhood (as defined by the American advertising industry) is a more powerful religious symbol for it than the Holy Spirit.

The only reasonable solution in such cases, it seems to me, is to preach the gospel with the full realization that the community to which one is preaching is also caught up, on that particular day, in the observance of a time that is determined by a calendar other than that of the church. If Mother's Day happens to fall on Pentecost, the preacher is not excused from announcing the great gift of God to his church and inviting the assembly to respond with faith and thanksgiving for the overflowing gift of God's love, which has been poured into our hearts. But this gospel may be proclaimed in such a way that the love of a mother for her family can be seen as a concrete and powerful expression of the love of God for us. The coincidence of secular observances with the calendar of the church year need not set up an either-or conflict. They rather provide the opportunity for the preacher to show how these human times and realities are also addressed by the word of God.

II. THE STRUCTURE
AND USE OF THE LECTIONARY

The revival of interest in the lectionary on the part of many Christian churches antedates the appearance of the Roman Catholic lectionary in Advent, 1971. However, because of the systematic way in which this lectionary was created, and the relative success of the venture, it was adopted by Presbyterians, Episcopalians, Lutherans, Methodists (working through the Consultation on Church Union), the United Church of Christ, and the Christian Church (Disciples of Christ) as the basis for the lectionaries that they proposed to their communities. Thus, the Roman Catholic lectionary became, as Methodist liturgical theologian James White describes it, "Catholicism's greatest gift to Protestant preaching, just as Protestant biblical scholarship has given so much impetus to Catholic preaching."[1]

The reasons that the lectionary has proven so popular are not difficult to find. Although there will undoubtedly never be a perfect lectionary, the extensive research and consultation that went into the formation of this one have made it a remarkably rich resource for the preaching and worship of Christian communities. Ministers and congregations are more easily able to plan in advance for their liturgical celebrations. Biblical and liturgical theologians can prepare materials to aid preaching and worship, and these materials can be further enriched to the degree that such endeavors are ecumenical in nature.[2] Preachers and people can meet (often in ecumenical settings) to pray over and discuss the scriptures in preparation for the liturgy of the coming Sunday or season. Above all, the lectionary contributes to make worship and preaching a cooperative work between clergy and laity by providing them with a common basis in the word of God from which their reflection and planning can proceed. Its importance for the renewal of preaching and worship suggests a detailed look at its origin, structure, and use.

VATICAN II AND THE LECTIONARY

The mandate that the Second Vatican Council gave to the Roman Catholic Church regarding the use of scripture in the liturgy was a very general one. The Constitution on the Liturgy simply stated: "In sacred celebrations there is to be more reading from Holy Scripture, and it is to be more varied and suitable" (#51). Although in itself such a directive does not necessarily imply the formation of a lectionary, that is, a predetermined selection of readings from scripture for each day or rite, there is little doubt that the fathers of the council had such an implementation of their directive in mind. They had so consistently spoken of the revision of liturgical *books*, and the emphasis of the constitution on "officially approved" forms of celebration was so strong, that there is little reason to think that "more varied and suitable" reading from scripture in the liturgy implied that Roman Catholic priests and communities were now invited to choose with total freedom the portions of the Bible that they would read for their liturgical celebrations.

Thus, when the Consilium, a post-conciliar commission to implement the liturgical directives of the council, was formed, it immediately thought in terms of a lectionary. However, rather than simply understanding its task to be an updating of the annual series of gospel and epistle lessons that had developed over a fifteen-hundred-year period, it accepted its mandate as a call to develop a new way of organizing the Bible for use in Christian worship.

The eighteen members of a special commission on the lectionary began their work in 1964, just one year after the promulgation of the Constitution on the Liturgy. The first task they undertook was a review of all the lectionaries of the Latin liturgies that came into being between the sixth and twelfth centuries, those of fifteen Oriental rites, and those which were currently in use in Protestant churches. In addition to this they surveyed and synthesized the scholarly work on the origins and development of the lectionary that had taken place over the past eighty years.

In the following year thirty biblical scholars were asked to present lists of the texts they thought should be publicly proclaimed in the liturgy. This list was then presented to pastoral theologians for their scrutiny and comment. Following this, the commission prepared the general principles according to which it would choose the texts to be used and the order in which they would be arranged. In 1967 a lectionary for Sundays, feast days, and ordinary days was published in manuscript form and circulated. Revisions were made on the basis of reactions received, and on November 28, 1971, the first Sunday of Advent, the use of the new lectionary became mandatory for the Roman Catholic Church.

Even this brief overview of the Commission's work leads one to agree with James White, who writes in his introduction to the COCU lectionary: "The Consilium for the Implementation of the Constitution on the Sacred Liturgy sought and heeded the advice of hundreds of liturgical scholars and biblical experts from all the churches of Christendom. If the resulting lectionary is not the perfect one, at least it is certainly the most carefully prepared in the history of Christianity."[3]

The fundamental principle guiding the work of the lectionary commission was that the lectionary would find its thematic unity in the Paschal mystery, which had been completed in Christ and is to be completed in us.[4] In arrriving at this decision the commission reiterated the basic emphasis of the Constitution on the Liturgy as a whole: it is the "blessed passion, resurrection from the dead, and glorious ascension of Christ" which has redeemed humanity and given perfect glory to God (#5). It thus rejected, at least implicitly, other ways of going about its task. The lectionary was not to be ordered around a "history of salvation" motif (understood as a line running from the creation to the second coming), or around a systematic presentation of the theological teachings of the church, or according to a literary analysis of the parts of the Bible that were to be used. Nor were the readings to be chosen and ordered for the primary purpose of exhorting and encouraging people to lead more Christian lives. The lectionary was there to proclaim the passion, death, resurrection, and ascension of Christ, fully realized in him and being realized in us who, through faith and baptism, have been joined to him.

Thus, in the choice of the Paschal mystery as the unifying theme of the lectionary, certain consequences were already indicated: the primary importance of the Sunday celebration, understood since earliest times as the celebration of the resurrection of Christ; the centrality of the Lenten-Easter season; a predilection for those passages of scripture which, in anticipation or remembrance, point to the person of Christ; and preaching understood primarily as the proclamation of the good news of what God has done for his people *(sola gratia, sola fide)* rather than as an exhortation to good works.

One of the first concrete decisions made by the commission was to return to the ancient custom of providing for three readings at the Sunday eucharist: a reading from the Old Testament, one from the Epistles, and one from the Gospels.[5] In arriving at this decision the commission was aware of the regularity with which the reading from the Old Testament had fallen into disuse in Christian worship. It also heard the objections of those who said that the Old Testament was too difficult to understand for ordinary people, and that three readings would make the liturgy of the word too long and too difficult to digest. However, in spite of these recognized difficulties, the decision to return to the early tradition was made, with the proviso that "for pastoral reasons" two instead of three readings could be used. It is worth noting, however, that it is not the Old Testament reading which is automatically to be dropped. Rather, if

> the conference of bishops decides to permit only two readings, one of the first two should be chosen which is of greater value in presenting the mystery of salvation to the faithful. Unless expressly stated otherwise in another part of the lectionary, it is preferable to choose the reading which is more closely related to the day's gospel, more helpful in presenting an organized and unified instruction over a period of time, or which permits a semi-continuous reading of a book of the Bible.[6]

The second major decision to be made was whether to go with a two-, three-, or four-year cycle. Although there were some consultants who argued in favor of continuing a one-year cycle because of the advantages, pastorally speaking, of the repetition of key scriptural texts, the members of the commission opted overwhelmingly in favor of a multiple-year cycle in order to provide "more lavish and richer" scriptural fare to the assembled congregations. A two-year cycle was judged to be insufficient to accomplish this end, and the four-year cycle was rejected because it would involve too many repetitions and would mean that the scriptural texts used for the liturgy of the hours would be taken from the less important sections of the Bible or would repeat those which had been assigned to the lectionary. The three-year cycle was seen to be ideal. Not only was the length of time adequate, but a three-year cycle also allowed for the provision of one of the Synoptic Gospels as the Gospel of the year for each of the three years. The Gospel of John would then be read primarily in the Lenten and Easter seasons, in accord with a long-standing liturgical tradition. Thus Matthew was assigned to year A, Mark to year B, and Luke to year C, the latter being defined as a year that is divisible by three.

The solution of a three-year cycle with a Gospel of the year is undoubtedly one of the most successful features of the lectionary. Each of the three years has its own character, determined by the emphasis of the individual Evangelist. This arrangement of the gospel lessons both supports and draws strength from the school of biblical criticism known as *Redaktionsgeschichte*. Each of the Gospels is recognized as coming out of a particular theological emphasis that accounts for the ways in which the oral and written tradition about Jesus is organized. Preachers who take seriously this theological/thematic unity of each of the Gospels will be able to preach with a greater sense of unity and purpose than they would if they were simply dealing with individual passages chosen from any one of the four Gospels. The choice of a Gospel of the year almost demands of preachers that they try to see the whole Christ from the point of view of one of the Evangelists, and then share that vision of the whole Christ with their congregations.

The next major decision facing the commission was how to choose the three readings for each of the Sundays of the year. The commission decided to use both the thematic and the semi-continuous methods of selecting texts. For the Sundays of the major liturgical seasons (Advent, Christmas, Lent, and Easter), as well as for major feast days of the sanctoral cycle, the readings were chosen with reference to the theme of the feast or season. Thus, for example, the gospel on the first Sunday of Advent always deals with the Lord's coming in glory at the end of time, those on the second and third Sundays with John the Baptist, and that on the fourth with the events that immediately prepared for the Lord's birth. The Old Testament readings for all the Sundays of Advent are prophecies about the Messiah and messianic times, and the selections from the writings of the Apostle present exhortations and instructions on different themes of the season.

For the Sundays of Pentecost it seemed most logical to employ a semi-continuous reading of the Gospel (that is, a *lectio continua* that allowed for certain omissions). The assignment of one of the Synoptic Gospels to each of the three years already implied such an ordered, continuous reading. In addition, the introduction of the Gospel in the Latin liturgy ("*Sequentia sancti evangelii* . . ."—"A continuation of the holy Gospel . . .") pointed back to an old tradition of reading the Gospel continuously.[7]

With regard to the Old Testament and epistle readings during Pentecost, however, the decision was a more difficult one. There were those who argued that both these lessons also be read continuously, but this solution was rejected by the majority of the commission who felt that three separate continuous readings would simply place too much strain on the attention of the listener, to say nothing of the demands placed on the preacher who would try to deal with three disparate texts in the homily. At the other extreme there were those who argued that all three readings should be harmonized with one another. This option was also rejected, at least insofar as it implied some kind of rigid and artificial systematization stemming from intellectual a prioris or rigid catechetical outlines.[8]

The solution finally arrived at was a compromise. The Old

Testament reading was chosen to parallel the gospel lesson for the day, the point of comparison being indicated by the summary sentence printed in italics at the head of each lesson. The rationale offered was that such a choice would make it more possible to grasp the totality of the history of salvation.[9] During the Easter season, when a lesson from the Acts of the Apostles is used in place of the Old Testament lesson,[10] there does not seem to have been any attempt to establish a parallel with the gospel lesson.

The second lesson, generally from the Letters of Paul, was, like the gospel, also read as a *lectio semi-continua*. The major exception to this rule was the decision to spread the reading of the First Letter to the Corinthians and the Letter to the Hebrews over three years. The commission decided that, given the length and variety of topics of First Corinthians and the theological density of the Letter to the Hebrews, it would be too taxing to read these letters through continuously in one year.

DIFFICULTIES WITH THE LECTIONARY

These two decisions—to harmonize the Old Testament reading with the gospel lesson and to treat the epistle as a *lectio semi-continua* without reference to the other two lessons—have evoked most of the negative criticism that has been directed at the lectionary. While it may be true that "lectionaries have always been subject to complaints,"[11] and that the complexities in fashioning a lectionary for the church today are such that "no completely satisfactory solution was possible,"[12] these specific decisions of the commission have been seen by some liturgical and biblical scholars as erroneous, if not in principle then at least in the manner in which they were implemented. Gerard Sloyan, for instance, writes that while the lectionaries rise "to laudable heights in establishing the correspondence between the two testaments, in ways that would have pleased the New Testament writers and the church fathers, they also tend to reduce the Hebrew revelation to a matter of little consequence apart from the fact of Jesus Christ."[13] Not only did the creators of the lectionary shy away from any sustained telling of any of the great tales, they seemed to be uneasy about including any problem raised in the Old Testament that was not, in some direct and clear way, "answered" by the revelation made in Jesus Christ. In short, the Old Testament is offered only as a foreshadowing of the Messiah, and not as a robust presentation of the many and various ways in which God inserted and continues to insert himself in human history and of the ways in which human beings accept and reject that divine presence. The way in which the Old Testament is used in the lectionary implies that *everything* in it needed to be either rejected or perfected by the coming of Christ. While such an approach may have been allowable in the first century, it is not to be entertained in the twentieth, "especially by churches that are busy saying they have learned something about the universality of the divine concern as the sum of religious particularities. It is one thing to affirm that Christ is to be found on every page of the Bible and another to prove it by a series of narrow correspondences that leaves room for little else."[14]

Those who object to the application of the *lectio semi-continua* principle for the choice of the epistle lesson claim that the lack of unity between the second reading, on the one hand, and the first and third, on the other, creates a "real and *insoluble* problem when it comes to the homily."[15] One author describes the situation as similar to driving down a superhighway. The Old Testament is traveling down lane one. But suddenly the lane is closed off and the epistle reading is signaled in. When it has run its course, it is taken off the road and lane one is opened again for the gospel.[16]

To show how difficult the situation can become, J. D. Crichton gives the example of the second Sunday in Pentecost, year C. The gospel for that Sunday is the account of the wedding at Cana, and the choice of Isaiah 62:1-5 as the Old Testament reading indicates that the compilers of the lectionary regarded the wedding motif as central, even though, as Crichton notes, exegetes would not agree that marriage is the central concern of the Cana account. But then we find that the epistle reading, from I Corinthians 12, deals with *charismata*, and we wonder what could possibly have been in the mind of the compilers. The explanation we receive is that I Corinthians begins on this Sunday in year A, is continued in year

B, with the remainder given over to year C. "This," he concludes, "is called *lectio continua!*"[17] It is because of the absence of any thematic unity to tie together all three lessons, he and others would claim, that the preacher must make an option for one or the other of these continuous streams of thought in working out the homily.

There can, I believe, be little doubt that these criticisms of the ways in which the authors of the lectionary dealt with the Old Testament and epistle readings indicate real difficulties in using the lectionary for preaching. Some of these difficulties have been alleviated by the revisions of the lectionary that were made by other Christian churches, but to a great extent they remain to be addressed by more extensive revisions in the future.

PREACHING FROM THE LECTIONARY

In spite of the fact that Vatican II called for a richer fare of scripture at the table of the Lord, it would not be appropriate to understand the primary purpose of the lectionary as introducing Christian worshipers to a greater familiarity with the Bible as such. If the principal purpose of the lectionary is to proclaim the Paschal mystery of Christ, then it inevitably follows that the lectionary is Christ-centered. This implies that the guiding principle behind the choice of Old Testament texts will not be to provide congregations with an appreciation of the dramatic intensity of Old Testament narratives, the richness of its poetic imagery, or the profundity of its presentation of the doubt and anguish that afflict the human heart. Nor will the Old Testament lessons be chosen to offer a panoramic presentation of the religious development of Israel. The purpose of the lectionary is not, to paraphrase the words of Reginald Fuller, to instruct the congregation in the history of religion, even of biblical religion. Rather, the lectionary is at the service of the proclamation of the word of God, which is Jesus Christ.[18]

To put this in other words, we can say that the use of the Old Testament in the lectionary and in the liturgy is, in fact, a *use* of it. It is to be hoped, of course, that this use will be enlightened, grounded in sound exegesis and freed from the compulsion to find conscious and explicit predictions of the life and meaning of Christ in every passage. But if the liturgy is primarily the common celebration of the coming of Christ, then it will be predisposed, as it were, to make use of those passages of the Old Testament which express the hope and longing of the Jewish people for a deeper and more profoundly transforming presence of God in human history. And, vice versa, it will tend to look on the Old Testament from the vantage point of life in Christ, through whom and in whom all the hopes and longings of the prophets have been radically, if not completely, fulfilled.[19]

To say this, of course, is not to provide a justification for the particular choices of Old Testament lessons that are currently to be found in the lectionary. In fact, it may be true to say that the christocentric principle would be better served by a fuller presentation of the great stories and figures of the Old Testament, rather than by so many prophetic oracles and ethical exhortations. And yet, might we not see in the heavy use of the Book of Isaiah in the lectionary, for instance, a harking back to the predilection of the New Testament authors for this book (along with the Book of Psalms) as they searched for ways to proclaim the person and meaning of Christ?

If the choice of the Old Testament lesson has been problematic for biblical scholars, it has not been so for most preachers. The fact that the Old Testament passage is chosen to harmonize with the gospel lesson for the Sundays in ordinary time means that the preacher can easily turn (all too easily, perhaps) to the Old Testament reading to reinforce or illustrate the central point of the gospel.

Preachers find greater difficulty with the second, or epistle lesson. A good number of them understand liturgical preaching to mean preaching that refers to and makes use of all the passages of scripture that have been read in a particular service. As long as these passages have all been chosen in the light of some unifying theme, as is the case on major feast days and the Sundays of the principal liturgical seasons, they have no great difficulty in doing this. But when they are confronted with a text that does not harmonize in a thematic way with the other lessons, they conclude that the only thing to do is read it, and then simply ignore it in the homily. Or they may consider using the dissonant text in another way. For instance, Adrian Nocent describes the possibility of reading the epistle as part of the introductory penitential service, and then structuring the penitential act around the theme of that reading. Even though he describes this use of the epistle as a "fairly good solution,"[20] I find it problematic in that it destroys the rhythmic structure of the liturgy of the word and gives entirely too much prominence to the penitential rite.

Although it would be possible in a future revision of the lectionary to choose the epistle reading according to the same principle of harmonization that is operative for the choice of the Old Testament reading, without thereby resorting to the rigid a priori model of harmonization that was so unequivocally rejected by the lectionary commission, I believe it is still possible to preach from the lectionary as we have it without either ignoring the second reading, or referring to it in an artificial and forced way. Let me indicate how I think this might be done.

Normally, I believe, you will begin to work from the gospel in preparing a homily. This practice is commended by liturgical tradition, which regards the proclamation of the gospel as the climactic moment of the liturgy of the word, as well as by the makeup of the lectionary itself, structured as it is around the gospel of the year. However, subsequent preparation for the homily should include frequent readings of all the scriptural texts of the liturgy. In this way you will be setting up for yourself a situation in which the scriptures will be read and heard alongside one another and thus, almost inevitably, serve to interpret one another. And, if any reminder be needed, one of the most traditional, and helpful, of hermeneutical principles is that scripture is its own best interpreter.

Thus, as you work with the gospel, and with the Old Testament lesson that corresponds to it, keep your eye on the epistle. Let it be there, on the horizon, in the background, lurking, as it were, in the shadows. As you read it—and multiple readings are absolutely necessary—in connection with the other texts, do not try to force it to relate to the gospel and Old Testament lesson. Simply let yourself be open to the ways in which this lesson can draw further meaning from the text of the gospel, can throw light on it, can be seen as indicating a way in which the Paschal mystery of Christ is being completed, or needs to be completed, in us. If you do this, you will, I believe, almost always be surprised and delighted by the unexpected insights you receive.

By way of example, let us look again at the lessons for the second Sunday of the year in year C: Isaiah 62:1-5, Psalm 96:1-2a, 2b-3, 7-8a, 9-10ac; I Corinthians 12:4-11; and John 2:1-12. If you remember, this set of pericopes was singled out as indicative of the major problems in the present lectionary: the choice of an Old Testament reading that harmonizes with the gospel, but does not necessarily correspond to what contemporary exegetes hold to be central in the particular gospel passage; an epistle reading that is on its own *lectio continua* track, and that, in this particular place, picks up the reading of an epistle that is spread over three years.

I have already indicated that although it is true that the gospel account is not a presentation of Jesus' teaching on marriage, or even in some indirect way, a sign of Jesus' blessing of marriage,[21] it does present marriage as a symbol of messianic fulfillment. Therefore, the choice of Isaiah 62:1-5, with its references to Israel's call to be the beloved bride of God, seems singularly appropriate.

But what are we to do with the selection from I Corinthians 12, which speaks of "varieties of gifts, but the same Spirit; . . . varieties of service but the same Lord" and which goes on to list the various manifestations of the Spirit: utterance of wisdom and knowledge, faith, gifts of healing, and the like? If the preacher has decided that the gospel text leads to a proclamation, in compelling, concrete, colorful ways, of the love of God for his people, of Jesus for his church, using the imagery and experience of married love to do this, and if, while working with these ideas and images, an eye is kept on the epistle, then I think something like this could happen. The epistle speaks of gifts and services and of the God who inspires them all in everyone. How does this inspiration come about? Is it not through love, through knowing and feeling that we are loved? What is it that releases those creative bursts of energy and enthusiasm and generosity in our lives? What makes us turn away from ourselves, from our narrow and selfish interests, and attend to the needs of others joyously and freely? Is it a command or a law? Is it a sense of obligation or duty? Hardly. It is rather the sense of being delighted in by someone else, of being rejoiced over, to pick up the phrases of the Isaian text. When that happens, we are free. The floodgates open, and the gifts and services spill out.

Thus, it seems to me, these three pericopes can provide a remarkable opportunity for authentic liturgical proclamation. We are here at the heart of the gospel: the love of God for his people, and what that love does to them. It makes them lovers. We are here at the heart of liturgical action: a community that turns to God in praise and thanksgiving for the wonders he has accomplished and the gifts he has given. And we are at the heart of Christian life: gifts and services rendered to others, not grudgingly and out of a sense of compulsion, but freely, out of a recognition of the overwhelming gifts of the Spirit of love that have been poured into our hearts by the Father through his Son Jesus.

These particular readings may have seemed to lend themselves especially well to demonstrate the point I am trying to make: that dealing with a double series of continuous readings does not necessarily mean the preacher is forced to ignore one or the other series, or to draw connections that are at best peripheral to the basic meaning of the texts or at worse fanciful, arbitrary, and artificial. But my reason for choosing them was not that I found them especially apt to prove my point. It was rather that they had been singled out as paradigmatic of the insurmountable difficulty of preaching from the lectionary as it is now composed. From my own experience of using the lectionary, I am confident that any set of pericopes would serve equally well as a basis for my argument.

Since the gospel usually serves as the basic text for the homily, I spoke of always keeping an eye on the epistle as one worked through the gospel and Old Testament lessons. But the process can be reversed if one chooses to preach from the epistle.[22] In this case, the recommendation of Reginald Fuller in a book written well before the appearance of the new lectionary is still timely:

If the Epistle is taken from the doctrinal portion of the epistles, the preacher's task will be to penetrate behind the doctrinal argumentation to the *kerygma* whose implications are being set forth, and to confront the congregation with that *kerygma* so that they might renew their response to it in faith preparatory to the Godward memorial of the liturgical action. And the Epistles from the paraenetic sections will demand a similar treatment. They are not to be used for little moralistic exhortations of the preacher's own. His task is rather to penetrate behind the paraenesis to the *kerygma* it presupposes, to confront the congregation with the *kerygma* so that it may be the occasion of a renewed encounter with Jesus Christ in the liturgy and thence to indicate the kind of behaviour that encounter will imply in the daily lives of the people in their contemporary situation. [23]

But whether one preaches from the gospel or the epistle as the primary text, it is always best to preach a *series* of homilies from one or the other continuous readings. To skip from gospel to epistle and back to gospel again runs counter to one of the basic principles behind the organization of the lectionary and will obviously not be a very effective way of communicating to the congregation a sense of direction and purpose in preaching.

To conclude this section, a visual model of the process I have been describing might be helpful. Think of the Old Testament and the gospel readings as the two bottom points of a triangle, and the epistle as the top. As you work with the gospel and the Old Testament, the epistle is hovering over you, calling you, as it were, to lift up the work you are doing to some higher synthesis, to see it from another perspective. In other words, do not think of the epistle as on the same horizontal line as the gospel and the Old Testament. It is, in some way, outside of the field. When it "reaches down" and picks up the strands of gospel and Old Testament, or when gospel and Old Testament "reach out" and "grab hold" of the doctrinal arguments or moral exhortations of the epistle, then you have the knot that ties together those parts of the scriptures and holds them in a creative tension that can come to expression in the word of preaching.

III. THE PASTORAL
USE OF THE LECTIONARY

In the introduction to their multi-volume anthology of Christian preaching, Clyde Fant and William Pinson write that over the centuries those preachers who exercised the greatest impact upon the world were those who spoke to the needs and issues of their day. [1] What could seem farther removed from this kind of preaching than the liturgical homily? In the first place, it is related to texts of scripture that have been assigned to specific days without any possible foreknowledge of the needs or setting of a particular congregation or the interests or capabilities of a particular preacher. Second, it is tied to a sequence of time and the celebrations of feasts that no longer have much impact on the societies in which we live.

For some people, the very idea of liturgical preaching conjures up an image of total irrelevance: priests dressed in outlandish clothes, who, after performing arcane rituals, address the initiates on such esoteric topics as Gelasian sacramentaries, Nicene creeds, Whitsuntide, antependia, Gregorian chant, epicleses, and responsorial psalms. We are obviously engaging in caricature here, but one that does point up a real difficulty. Liturgical preaching can all too easily become so concerned with pericopes, rites, and seasons, and so limit itself to explanatory comments and exegetical interpretation, that it loses sight of the people to whom it is addressed and thereby becomes radically irrelevant and ultimately dismissed as pious twaddle. Or, what may be even worse, it attracts to itself a coterie of churchy types who find a kind of pathetic delight in all the frills and paraphernalia of ecclesiastical ritual.

In a strict sense of the term it may be true that liturgical preaching is preaching that explains the symbolism of rites and feasts by means of reference to biblical types. [2] When such preaching is done well, it can indeed serve to show how the rites and feasts of the church do have a "vital meaning for ordinary Christians today."[3] But it is difficult to see how preaching conceived primarily as an explanation of rites and feasts by means of their biblical types, even when the preacher attempts to relate them to daily living, can be heard by most congregations today as a word of vital importance. The people who gather for worship do so, it seems, not primarily to learn about the Bible or about the scriptural basis for the rites and ordinances of the church, but rather to hear a word that they hope will be directed to them in their concrete circumstances and will help them find some meaning and purpose in their lives. It may well be that it is precisely in the bath of regeneration or in the breaking and sharing of the bread that this meaning will be revealed, but in order to hear that, they need first to know that *they* are heard, that their situation is recognized and understood.

And what is this situation of theirs? According to a study made by Edgar Jackson some years ago, which still rings true today, in the average parish congregation about one fifth of the people will be feeling a sense of loss because of a recent bereavement. A third of them may be facing marital difficulties. About half of them will have problems of adjusting emotionally to school, job, home, or community. Others will be afflicted with a deep sense of guilt stemming from their inability to deal maturely with their sexuality, or because of their addiction to drugs or alcohol.[4]

Preachers and others who sense the immediacy and immensity of these problems are understandably impatient with preaching that does not attend to them. These are the real issues, they say, and they need to be dealt with. If the scriptures or the liturgy in general get in the way, then they have to be left aside, in order, as one person put it, that the preacher may tackle instead "a controversial and timely subject which affects the spiritual and moral well-being of his flock." This is, so the thinking goes, certainly to be preferred to the situation in which "the preacher first puzzles over the Scriptural reading for the coming Sunday, asks himself what it means to him and his flock, and then launches out into the deep with his sermon for better or worse."[5]

Enough of these irrelevant liturgical homilies, say the critics. Vital sermons on pressing contemporary social concerns are what we need. A Roman Catholic priest in Minneapolis writes on the editorial page of one of the city's daily papers:

> See if you can find an advertised Sunday sermon dealing with a red-hot controversial issue. Do you see anything there about the capitalistic crunch, the immorality of arming for nuclear war, the harsh and unholy restriction of the rights of women, galloping racism, our brutal penal system, neglect of the elderly? Look again. Get a magnifying glass. The continuing clockwork orange, the violence exercised by powerful institutions, the madness increasing as machines grow larger, man's inhumanity to man in the marketplace—these striking themes rarely receive a mention, much less a message. Consolation for the congregation is considered essential; a call to radical change or heroic holiness is muted.[6]

There is no denying that these concerns are real, at times overwhelming, and need to be addressed by those in the Christian community who have been called to exercise the role of pastor and preacher. Nor, I think can there be any serious disagreement with Father Egan's insistence that the liturgical assembly is one of the arenas in which this address can and should be made. The challenge to preachers if to find ways to address these problems and concerns not only with their own words but with the word of God, a word that is read and heard in its full sweep and scope. The challenge is also to preach this word in such a way that it enables the people to enter more fully into the liturgical action for which they have gathered, and to go forth from it strengthened for the task at hand. In other words, liturgical preaching is not at all an alternative to preaching that deals with red-hot controversial issues, or which opts for consolation rather than a call to radical change or heroic holiness. But, for the preacher who is willing to be guided by the whole message of the scriptures that the lectionary offers, it can provide an alternative to the single-issue, moralistic harrangues that are sometimes justified in the name of relevant, "prophetic" preaching.

If we are to believe that the lectionary and the liturgy can be a

source of preaching that not only comforts but also challenges the
faithful, it means, of course, that we begin with the conviction that
the scriptures and the liturgy are not, in themselves, at odds with or
out of touch with what is human. In fact, it means that we see in the
scriptures a continual attempt to wrestle with the very meaning of
human existence at the level of depth, and that we accept the New
Testament's presentation of Jesus as the one in whom the deepest
meaning of human existence is revealed. And finally it means that
we regard the liturgy as the ongoing reappropriation of this meaning
through contact with Jesus by means of word and ritual action. This
understanding of scripture and liturgy indicates, I believe, that
preaching which flows from the scriptures and is rooted in the liturgy
is the preeminent means for dealing not just with the symptoms and
external manifestations of human misery, but with its root causes.

This concern to address the source and cause of human suffering
is at the very center of effective and responsible preaching. A
rationale for this kind of preaching and a detailed method for
accomplishing it can be found in Milton Crum's *Manual for
Preaching.*[7] There he shows that to deal only with symptoms and
manifestations is faulty on a number of counts: such preaching does
not affect our image of the world, the way we see things; and it is out
of our image (or to put it more theologically, out of our faith in the
ways things are) that our actions flow. Second, it makes the Bible, at
least good parts of it, irrelevant, because the manifestations and
symptoms of sin, although often strikingly similar, are by no means
the same now as they were two or three thousand years ago. And
third, it fails to see that the Bible itself is concerned to provide an
interpretation of the human situation, to explain why we are the way
we are, and what we can do about it—or better, what God has done
and is doing about it.

But how do we get at the roots of the condition we find ourselves
in? There is certainly no one way, and the preacher who has access to
a number of them is certainly in a privileged position. There is the
way of the philosopher, who reflects on thought and language and
the ways in which humans have dealt with such questions as the
good and the true. There is the way of the social scientist, who by

studying social organizations, cultural patterns, or psychological processes is able to move back into the realms of personal and collective unconscious or into the dim recesses of human memory. There is certainly the way of the artist, who by means of the well chosen word, the shape of a line or a melody, or the shading of a color, is able to put us in touch with our deepest thoughts and feelings and thereby help us to own and order them that their energy may be productive rather than damaging to us and our environment.

But there is also (dare we say especially?) the way of the preacher, who, through loving study of the scriptures and loving contact with people, is able to hear the scriptures as a word of profound significance for people's lives and is then able to give expression to that word in language that people understand and respond to.

So we come, again and always, to the preacher as mediator, as the one who stands as a bridge between congregation and scripture, enabling them the more easily to interact. The preacher is one who, through personal gift and professional training, is able to hear both the people and the scriptures on the level of depth, and who is then able to bring these two words together into dialogue and forward into worship and obedience. The question, of course, is how?

THE SCRIPTURES FIRST

The normal way for the liturgical preacher is to begin with the scriptures that have been assigned to a particular day. This is not the only way to preach from the scriptures, as is obvious from a long tradition in many Protestant churches of not using a lectionary. But, in a certain sense, neither is it the only way for the liturgical preacher. The preaching that takes place on special occasions, whether these be tied to a calendar, a community observance, or a particular situation of need or rejoicing, are the most obvious instances of what I am talking about. For instance, in the Roman Catholic lectionary, after the readings for the temporal and the sanctoral cycles, we find the following classifications:

Ritual Masses—lessons for the celebration of the sacraments, for funerals, and for rites connected with the vows of poverty, chastity, and obedience.

Masses for Various Occasions—under this heading come four subheads:

1. For the Church (e.g., for the election of a pope or bishop, for the unity of Christians, for pastoral or spiritual meetings);
2. For Civil Needs (for peace and justice, in time of war and civil disturbance);
3. For Various Public Needs (e.g., beginning of the new year, after the harvest, for the sick, in thanksgiving);
4. For Particular Needs (for forgiveness of sins, for a happy death).

The provision of numbers of alternate scriptural texts for these special times and needs is a clear indication that at times the actual situation of a worshiping community is of such an intense nature that it will determine what scriptures are to be appropriately read on that occasion.

In speaking about eucharistic celebrations for special groups, the General Instruction on the Order of Mass[8] says that the "priest may choose from the readings of that week those most suitable for the group" (#319). The American Roman Catholic bishops decided that even more latitude should be allowed on such occasions. In a decision taken on November 13, 1969, they agreed to permit the "choice of readings not found in the current week, provided they are within the approved lectionary, are appropriate to the particular celebration, and are not chosen to the disadvantage of the ordinary use of the weekday lectionary."[9]

A couple of comments are in order. First of all, we should note that the official directives of even the Roman Catholic Church make provision for the choice of appropriate texts on special occasions. The Roman liturgy is among the most minutely regulated of all liturgical traditions. If it allows for a choice of texts, Christians who come from a less closely regulated liturgical tradition need hardly fear that the adoption of a lectionary will limit them, once and for all, to assigned texts.

Second, we should note that the General Instruction restricts itself to weekdays when speaking of the possibility of choosing texts for the celebration of a eucharist. This, I believe, is a wise restriction. The Sunday gathering is, by definition, the gathering of the entire Christian community, and it is proper that the liturgy on that day not be centered on some particular occasion or issue. Nonetheless, it is obvious that there will be those occasions when the Sunday celebration will coincide with an event, whether catastrophic or benign, of such proportions that an unyielding attachment to the lectionary could only be interpreted as scrupulous legalism or pastoral insensitivity. On these occasions, rare as they may be, the only appropriate response is to choose passages from the scriptures that speak directly and powerfully to the situation, if such passages are to be found. In any event, if the situation is of such importance that you must speak to it directly, and if the pericopes assigned for that particular day do not provide you with an appropriate word, no matter how diligently you have sought to hear one there, then by all means choose readings that do enable you to preach the word of the Lord. But do not (repeat, do not) read the lessons from the lectionary and then ignore them completely in your preaching. To do so is a clear, indeed eloquent, way of informing the congregation that the liturgy is something we do because we have to, but that it really doesn't have anything to do with life. You may insist that this is not the way you regard the liturgy, and you may continue to repeat all sorts of wonderful statements from the Constitution of Vatican II about the liturgy being the "outstanding means by which the faithful can express in their lives, and manifest to others, the mystery of Christ and the real nature of the true Church" (#2), but your words will not be able to withstand the eloquence of your actions, which proclaim that you really believe the liturgy is simply a ritual prelude to the sermon, in which, finally, the real issues and concerns of the people can be met.

In saying that the preaching should flow out of the lessons read, rather than out of a separate sermon text, I do not "postulate that the bringing to life of written words can only be effected by preaching about them," a position strongly rejected by von Allmen, who insists that the liturgical reading of the scriptures is more than simply a prelude to preaching.[10] I too believe that in the very reading of the scriptures Christ is present. My point is not so much that the scriptures need to be preached to be received as the word of God, but that the homily needs to be rooted in the scriptures that have been read if it is to be an integral element of the liturgical action and not simply a talk on a scriptural text or a religious topic that is inserted into the service.

DWELLING WITH THE WORD

We now return to the regular "week-in, week-out"[11] preaching which constitutes the major part of the pastor's preaching ministry. How is it possible to combine a sensitivity for the rhythm of the liturgical year, the use of predetermined texts, and a concern for the needs and questions of the people to whom one is ministering in a course of regular Sunday preaching?

For the preacher who uses a lectionary, the question at the beginning of a week is not, What am I going to preach about next Sunday?—a question usually asked with a certain degree of anxiety, if not panic—but, more simply, What are the lessons for next Sunday? Even that question will be answered in part before it is asked, for the preacher will no doubt know from which of the Evangelists the gospel will be taken and may even remember which of the Letters of Paul is currently being read.

At any rate liturgical preaching begins with the scriptures, in particular the scriptural lessons appointed for a certain day of the year. Thus the preacher's primary obligation is not to solve people's problems or answer their questions, but to hear the scriptures as God's living word, and then to communicate that word so that others may hear it as well and be drawn to respond to it.

How does this hearing take place? It occurs when we dwell with the word, allowing it to become familiar to us and in so doing to surprise us with its newness and relevance. This "dwelling with the word" is the first and indispensable step in preaching it. Unless we hear the word, there is very little likelihood that we will speak it in a way that others will be able to hear it as a word of life for them. It will be simply "information," interesting perhaps, but most likely boring and irrelevant. Something from "back then" and "out there," which has no meaning for their lives. As Kierkegaard rightly noted, there is no lack of information in the land, but information is not what saves.[12]

"Dwelling with the word" implies the sort of reading of the scriptures that is at the very heart of patristic and monastic spirituality. This "spiritual reading" (*lectio divina*) is done for formation rather than information. It is slow, meditative reading that cares not a whit about getting through a passage or a book. Nor is it especially concerned with questions about the authorship or history of the text. Rather it is reading that takes the text as it is given and waits patiently on it, allowing it to question, affirm, challenge, or comfort the reader.

This kind of reading works best of all with texts that are familiar, the classic texts of a particular religious or cultural tradition. We go to such texts not expecting to find new information (will the Samaritan stop or won't he?), but rather in the hope of hearing a familiar word in a new way. It had never struck us the way it strikes us now. It had never seemed so real, so right, so immediate. The text hasn't changed, but we have, and we hear it now in a way that convinces us that God is speaking to us, offering us a word of life.

But how do we arrive at such a hearing of the word? First of all, it must be affirmed that there are no surefire tricks for bringing this about. The hearing of God's word, as with every other human contact with the divine, is purely and utterly a matter of God's gracious gift. If we hear his word, it is because he chooses to speak. And that speaking can take place at any time and through any means.

But while we can never manipulate God, we can and must dispose ourselves to receive him, to hear the word. Furthermore, as Christians we share a common faith that the Bible is the record of the word that God has already spoken, indeed spoken once for all. To go to that written record with the hope that it may become a word for us, in our time and situation, is surely not manipulating God, but rather receiving gratefully the gift that he has already given and responding to it effectively.

And so we turn to the lessons from which we are to preach, and we read them. We read them again and again and again. Slowly, prayerfully. We let the word sink in. We read the word in different translations, not in the hope of finding some clever choice of words that we can capitalize on in our homily, but simply to allow the word as many entries into our mind and heart as possible. And if we have the good fortune to be able to read the texts in Greek or Hebrew, however haltingly, we go to the original texts. Again, we do so not so much in the hope of making some revolutionary discovery that till the present had eluded every exegete, and with which we will be able to dazzle the biblical scholar who just might happen to be in the congregation, but simply to allow a fuller dwelling with the word. This deeper contact with the word can happen when one knows the language hardly at all, when it is necessary to go to the dictionary for every second or third word and to check back in the grammar to find out whether that aorist is middle or passive. Such attention to individual words, and the forms of those words, can frequently alert us to a nuance, or even an emphasis, which we had never noticed before, because we were reading along all the while quite sure of what was in that passage we had read so many times before.

THE DIFFICULT TEXT

As you ruminate on these texts, you will very likely find that there is a word or verse or passage that is especially troublesome. The reasons for this may be that you simply do not understand what the author is getting at. On the other hand, you may understand all too well! Or it may be that the word sounds totally irrelevant or even offensive when placed vis-à-vis the particular people and the specific situations you have to deal with. The temptation, of course, will be to skip over these passages, to look for something that seems more appropriate, more suited to the situation at hand. But don't do it! Stay with that difficult passage. Wrestle with it, not letting it go until it gives you an answer. The very reason it may be troubling you is that it wants to tell you something you may not want to hear, but something that is true and necessary for you nonetheless. It may be the "bad news" you need to hear before you can hear the good news of God's word.

In other words, don't fall into the trap of knowing in advance what the word of God will and should say to you. It is an easy trap to fall into.

> When a minister reads out of the Bible, I am sure that at least nine times out of ten the people who happen to be listening at all hear not what is really being read but only what they expect to hear read. And I think that what most people expect to hear read from the Bible is an edifying story, an uplifting thought, a moral lesson.[13]

And isn't this, more or less, what the preacher expects of a text for a sermon?

But if you are that sure you know what is to be found in the scriptures, then don't bother to use the lectionary at all. Simply go to the Bible and pick the passage that fits the particular message you have worked out. Do that, however, and you run the risk of shaping the word of God to your prejudices and limited vision. Let the word question you, challenge you, disturb you, as well as comfort and affirm you. Let it question your most basic convictions about "the way things are." Unless you are willing to do that, you really have not accepted the words of the prophet who has God say,

> For my thoughts are not your thoughts
>   neither are your ways my ways, says the Lord.
> For as the heavens are higher than the earth,
>   so are my ways higher than your ways
>   and my thoughts than your thoughts. (Isa. 55:8-9)

So stay with the difficult text, think about it, study it, pray over it, because it is out of those texts that your best preaching is going to come. It is from such troublesome verses that you are going to hear a new word of the Lord that will speak to your deepest needs and those of the people you will be addressing, those "existential concerns about survival and guilt and the meaning of their lives,"[14] concerns that are hardly ever touched by the sermons of preachers who know in advance what they are going to say. It is precisely the fact that we don't know in advance what we are going to say that makes liturgical preaching such a challenging and at the same time such an exhilarating enterprise. We come to a text of scripture bearing in our minds and hearts the concerns of a particular Christian community. What that text will say to these people remains to be seen—or shall we say, remains to be heard? We wait for a word from the Lord.

That waiting can be a rather nerve-racking business. It may well happen that as Sunday draws near, the problematic text remains just that. You have a lot of information about it, but it still doesn't say anything. You will again be tempted to drop it, to go with something tried and true, something familiar. But don't do it. Trust in the power of your nonconscious mental processes, or better, trust in the power of God working through them to draw forth from the relationship of troublesome text and existential concern a word that will speak to you and through you to God's people.

But what if that word doesn't come? What if you wake up Sunday morning still feeling that you have nothing to say? Well, consider the possibility that you will say nothing, that following the reading of the scriptures there will simply be a time of quiet before the gifts are brought to the altar and the eucharistic prayer begun. Not preaching when there is no word to speak is, I believe, an option that preachers must be willing to consider seriously.

And yet, even though I do believe we should remain open to the possibility that on a particular day we will honestly feel we have nothing to say and therefore remain quiet, I believe just as strongly that we need not worry about having something to say if we stay with the difficult verses of a text rather than those that are more familiar and immediately intelligible as we prepare to preach. Working from such difficult texts involves us, first of all, in a conscious and baffled struggle to find meaning, and then frequently in a sense of despair and a readiness to give up. But it is precisely such an attitude of turning away and pulling back that allows the nonconscious parts of our mind to go to work and bring about the flash of insight out of which the homily will grow.

This approach to the creative process, as applicable to the creation of a homily as to any other product of human intelligence, was developed by Harold Rugg in a book entitled *Imagination*. He himself offered the following summary statement of his theory:

> There is first a long, *conscious* preparatory period of baffled struggle; second, an interlude in which the scientist or artist apparently gives up, pushes the problem back or down or "out of mind," leaving it for the nonconscious to work upon. Then, third, comes the blinding and unexpected "flash of insight," and it comes with such certitude that a logical statement of it can be immediately prepared.[15]

Let us see how this understanding of the creative process might be applied to the movement from scriptural text to liturgical homily.

FROM TEXT TO HOMILY

As I suggested, the preacher who uses a lectionary will go to the texts for the following Sunday and read them through, prayerfully and meditatively, keeping in mind the particular people who will hear the homily. This reading should begin on Sunday evening and should continue through the week. Do everything you can to stay close to the texts. Read them aloud, check different translations, work on the original. But stay with the texts. Do not, at this point in the process of preparation, go to the commentaries or to any of the multitude of homiletic aids. You will be tempted to do this, especially if you find something that is particularly difficult or troubling in a text. But trust in your own ability to hear and understand. Don't let someone else tell you what the text means. The text is speaking to *you*, to you as an individual and to you as a representative of the community. Only you can hear what it is saying here and now. Don't be worried that you are going to make some foolish error in interpretation. You stand within a living tradition, and from this tradition you have inherited a way of approaching the scriptures that is so much a part of you that you may not even recognize it. Furthermore, your formal studies in the field of scripture and theology are a safeguard against error. Finally, the church's willingness to authorize you as a preacher is a clear sign that, because of character and training, you are judged to be responsible in your handling of the scriptures. So stay with the difficult text, struggle with it, pray with it, chew on it. Speak to it and let it speak to you.

Sometime in the middle of the week the time does come for checking the commentaries. You will want to consult the scholars not so much to get their ideas and their interpretation, as to make sure that you have not missed the main point of what the text is saying. You may, of course, also find help in the commentaries to support the idea you are working with. The fact that you go to the commentators at this point in the process of preparation, however, means that you will already have some ideas of your own about how the text is to be understood and you will therefore be able to judge what is of value in the materials that you now consult.

From midweek until Friday is the time for letting go, for allowing the process of incubation to take place. Try to forget about the fact that you are going to be preaching on Sunday, although you will really not be able to do this. You will find that your reading and listening, and especially your praying during these days will be directed and shaped by the texts that you are not consciously attending to. You will hear and see things in a way you wouldn't have heard and seen them before. You will notice what you might have otherwise ignored. And much of this material may find its way into your preaching as concrete instances of how the human situation is penetrated and transformed by the love of God.

And then comes Friday, when you should set aside a couple of hours to work on the homily. Frankly, these couple of hours always fill me with a kind of dread, or, if dread is too strong a word, then at least with a nervous anxiety. Although I have the time blocked out in my schedule (it took me years to discover that I had to block out time for myself if I was to have it), I find that I am always telling myself that I really have something more important to do. Or I find that I give in to all sorts of little distractions that keep me from my desk: the rug needs vacuuming, the picture frames haven't been dusted in months, I should spend a couple of minutes paging through *Time* before I get started just in case there is something there that I could use, and on and on.

I used to become quite upset with myself because of my inability to sit down and get right to work. But over the years I have come to recognize that this is simply the kind of game I have to play before I can settle in. These distractions don't really prevent me from getting to work on the homily; they are part of the process, a kind of dance before the doors of my mind on which I am soon going to knock to ask if "homily" can come out now.

And then finally I do sit down, pull out a sheet of paper, put it in the typewriter, and . . . I still don't have any idea what I am going to say. But I begin typing anyway, saying all the obvious things I know I am not going to use, but putting them down on paper even if only to dispose of them properly.

And then, more often than not, it happens. In the very act of writing the things I know I am not going to say, the idea comes. I hear, I understand, I see something that hadn't occurred to me before. Now I do know what I am going to say. I sense an excitement over the discovery of something new. There is a feeling of "So this is what that text is trying to say. Of course. Why didn't I see it before?" And along with that recognition comes a sense of gratitude, of thanksgiving, and the assurance that if I can share this vision of the way things are with the people who will hear this homily, then they too will be led to give praise and thanks to God, who offers them help and healing.

So I begin writing again, not concerned with finding the right words or turning a phrase nicely, or having all the points in their logical order. That can come later (it's only Friday, remember?). I write, as Francis McNutt says, "without the brakes on."[16] This is not the time to write a sentence, read it over, decide that it isn't quite right, scratch it out, and try to come up with something better. Revision comes later; you have all day tomorrow for that. Now is the time simply to write, to get it all out.

However, there will be times when it won't go quite so well. You will come to the end of the hour or two that you have set aside on Friday for writing the homily and feel as frustrated as when you began. No flash of insight will have come. Your time, however, has not been wasted. The idea needs more coaxing, and that's what you have been doing. You will have to let it sit a little longer, give it another try tomorrow, the time you normally would have used for rewriting and polishing. Don't worry that you are going to be cutting down on the time for the fine honing of the homily. Better a significant thought, roughly expressed, than old platitudes finely dressed. And if the idea still does not come on Saturday . . . well, there is still Sunday morning. And if it doesn't come then? Then, as I suggested, that may be the Sunday when there simply will not be a homily. But, provided you have begun the process early enough, so that there is sufficient time for incubation, those Sundays will be virtually nonexistent. The nice thing about the nonconscious dimension of the creative process is that it works on its own. If we give it the time, it will bring together those ideas that are clashing with one another and fashion them into insight.

LITURGICAL AND TOPICAL PREACHING

What makes liturgical preaching different from topical preaching? Two things: first of all, liturgical preaching generally begins from texts of scripture assigned for a particular day or a particular liturgical celebration. This is not the exclusive pattern, but it is the normal one. The scriptures guide us in recognizing both the misery and the grandeur of the human situation. Second, the liturgical homily specifies that the word to be addressed to that human situation is one that will enable the hearer to participate more fully in the liturgical action in which the preaching takes place. Thus, if the liturgical action is eucharistic, the homily will make use of the scriptures to interpret the human situation in such a way that the hearers can recognize the loving presence of God in their lives and turn to him with praise and thanksgiving and the joyful reception of his body and blood in communion. If the liturgical action is a service of reconciliation, the homily will be spoken as a word that invites and enables people to be forgiven and to forgive. And so on for baptism, for a service of healing, for the celebration of marriage. The liturgical homily is, in effect, an enabling word. It leads the hearer to faith, to a recognition of the way in which God is powerfully and lovingly present in our lives, and through this faith, to a richer, more personally involving participation in the celebration at hand. It is preaching that is concerned not so much to provide people with a word that will be useful for their behavior or their active involvement in the world of business and politics, though that concern is not absent, but rather, in the words of von Allmen, "to make the history of salvation become the story of their lives as well."[17] If this can be done, if people can recognize in their lives the presence of a God who continues to lead people out of darkness into light, continues to raise the dead, continues to call and equip people for discipleship, then they will find no action or attitude more appropriate than worship. And in that very act of praise and thanksgiving they will discover that they are built up and fitted out for lives of Christian service in the world.

PREACHER AND PASTOR

As may be quite evident, the method I have described for moving from scriptural text to homily presupposes that the preacher stands in a pastoral relationship to the congregation. I speak of pastoral relationship rather than pastoral office because there are those situations in which the preacher will not necessarily be the pastor of the worshiping community. For the preacher to stand in a pastoral relationship means, above all, that the preacher knows the community (see John 10:14—"I am the good shepherd; I know my own and my own know me"), is familiar with them on a personal level. At the very least, it means that the preacher has some understanding of human nature, of the way people think and act and feel.

Of course, in the normal week-in, week-out situations, the pastor and preacher are one and the same person, and therefore, when the scriptures are read in preparation for the homily, they are read by a person who knows and loves the community that will be hearing them read publicly on Sunday. In the end this pastoral relationship provides the best kind of audience analysis for liturgical preaching. As Barth put it, the adaptation of preaching to the congregation can only be based on love, which leads the preacher to "live the life of the congregation" and brings it about that "the question of what their thoughts really are is always in his mind."[18]

While the interaction of the preacher with the community through such normal pastoral means as personal counseling, the sacrament of reconciliation, or visits to people's homes will provide that kind of knowledge of the "audience" which is essential for effective communication, it would certainly be advantageous for the preacher to make use of some of the more sophisticated means described by communication theorists to determine in a more refined way the characteristics of the people who make up the congregation, their interest in and knowledge of the subjects of Christian preaching, and their basic attitudes, beliefs, and values. A questionnaire might be one way to gather such information, but the danger with such an instrument is that, in spite of our best attempts to explain the purpose of a survey of this kind, some people will inevitably regard it as a means of control and oppression. A better means might be to organize several small group discussions with a random sample of the parish in which people could be invited to talk about their satisfaction or frustration with the preaching they have heard and to present their suggestions for topics and areas to be dealt with. Such a discussion may need a good deal of structure on the part of the preacher if it is not simply to result in the predictable but all too general requests that sermons be more interesting and practical, or with the all too specific requests for sermons to provide answers to particular problems. In fact, while such groups may be invited for the specific purpose of improving preaching, they would very likely be much more helpful to the preacher if the discussions were not centered on preaching itself, but rather on more general issues and concerns. In this way the preacher would be given the opportunity to observe the clarity, salience, coherence, and integration of the images that are operative in the group,[19] and to get a handle on such matters as the taboos and formal requirements to be observed, the conventional beliefs and values that apply, and the factors that will operate to affect the long-range outcome of the preaching ministry.[20]

While the gathering of such *ad hoc* discussion groups can be extremely helpful to a preacher who is beginning a ministry in a particular church, there can be no doubt that the most valuable and effective means for a preacher to know a community and to judge the effectiveness of preaching in bringing the word of God to bear on the needs and issues of a particular congregation is through a structure by which the preacher meets regularly with members of the congregation to prepare for and review the regular Sunday preaching. For such groups to be most effective they should not be too large (four to six participants would be ideal), rotating (for example, with a new member coming on each week and staying on for four weeks), and as representative as possible of the entire community. This means that efforts may have to be made to get others than the predictable "joiners" to participate.

The best time for such a group to meet would be after one of the Sunday services. The first ten minutes or so of the session could be devoted to comments on the homily in light of the previous week's meeting. Then about twenty minutes could be given to an exegesis of the lessons for the coming Sunday, it being understood that these lessons would have been read in advance by all. Finally about a half an hour of the discussion would be devoted to dealing with the human situations that would seem to be addressed by these texts of scripture. Preachers who make use of such a method of preparation will find they have access to an effective instrument of audience analysis that would be the envy of any public speaker. This forum will provide them with a means of informal conversation with representative audience members that will allow them to become more fully informed about the specific concerns of the community and their ability and readiness to hear the preached word as a response to those concerns. In a more general way, the preacher will come to have a much more accurate picture of the image system of the auditors. Unless this picture is in place, the speaker "cannot fully understand what he is saying to the auditor when he makes any statement, whether calculated to produce some particular effect or not."[21]

It has been said that the greatest hindrance to effective communication is the presumption that it has taken place. The homily preparation group is a most effective way for the preacher to test out this presumption. You need to know what the people are thinking and saying, even if it is to disagree with them, to say that they too stand under the judgment of God's word and must turn away from their sins if they want to find life. The harsh and demanding words of the gospel will always fall on some rocky ground. But if the preacher is willing to listen, to learn, to come to know the people, it is quite possible that the word will be sown where it is more likely to take root and grow.

IV. PREACHING AND SACRAMENT

In both the Protestant and the Roman Catholic traditions of worship, the integral relationship between preaching and liturgy has not been very well maintained. Older Roman Catholics will still remember the days when it was not uncommon for the priest to remove his chasuble before proceeding to the pulpit for the Sunday sermon, thereby giving quite clear visible expression to the understanding that the sermon was an interruption of the mass. Those were, in fact, the days when the "real" beginning of the mass was placed at the offertory, when the bread and the wine were "offered" to God before they were consecrated. This being the case, legalistically inclined churchgoers could arrive after the "foremass," as the liturgy of the word was then called, and still consider themselves to have fulfilled their Sunday obligation. The reading of the scriptures and the preaching were considered to be prelude to the essence of the mass, which was the making present and sacrificial offering to the Father of the body and blood of Christ.

In the Protestant tradition—and here too I generalize and exaggerate—the situation was just the opposite. It was the sermon that was the central and all-important feature of the service of worship. All else was "setting" designed to show off the gem that the preacher had polished and perfected during the preceding week. Prayers, hymns, anthems, and lessons prepared the audience for the moment when the houselights would be dimmed, the pulpit illuminated, and the preacher would rise to announce the text and launch into a half-hour display of current commentary, verbal dexterity, and biblical expertise designed to entertain, enlighten, and inspire. When the sermon was over there was little left to do except leave a contribution, perhaps sing a concluding hymn, receive the blessing, and leave. Liturgy was thus reduced to the level of introduction and wrap-up, and perceived as such by many. For instance, a North of Ireland journalist is reported to have described a local church service by commenting, "The curate having finished the preliminaries, the Rector delivered himself of an eloquent discourse."[1]

Although the situation in both Protestant and Catholic communities has changed considerably, remnants of this tradition still remain. If, for some reason or other, time is limited, the Catholic priest instinctively thinks of abbreviating or eliminating the sermon as a way of shortening the service. Rare is the Roman Catholic Church in which the homily is seen as a normal element of every eucharistic service, and indeed of every sacrament, and not just of the Sunday eucharist, when it is mandatory. Protestant churches continue to print sermon titles in the newspaper and to display them on billboards in front of the church, thereby reinforcing the conviction that it is the sermon which is the central element of Christian worship. And, much more seriously, I believe, many Protestant churches continue to regard the eucharist not as the normal form of worship for the weekly gathering of Christians, but as a monthly or quarterly appendage to a preaching service.

I trust that Protestant readers of this volume will interpret these remarks not as the self-righteous criticisms of an outsider, but as the observations of a separated brother in Christ who hopes that through the renewal of preaching in the Roman Catholic Church and the recovery of the eucharist as the normative form of worship in Protestant Churches, we will more quickly come to the day when as brothers and sisters in Christ, we may offer the word of God to one another and share together in the table of the Lord. In order to accomplish this, we both need to recognize the essential interconnection between preaching and sacrament, a connection given forceful expression by von Allmen, who says:

> If we disqualify preaching in favour of the sacrament we also compromise the sacrament, since it then becomes a mechanical piece of magic, a human attempt to seize grace and become master of it. If we disqualify the

sacrament in favour of the sermon, we also compromise the sermon, because then it loses the reference which is necessary for its message, the outward commemoration of what it is announcing to us, and becomes the mere expression of an idea, with no power to grip us.[2]

Much the same point is made by Bernard Cooke, a Roman Catholic theologian, with the important observation that "preaching is limited neither to the occasion of liturgy nor to the content and style of the homily."[3]

Before continuing any further, it might be good to pause for a moment to consider this word "sacrament," which I have frequently used almost as a synonym for liturgy, and which is so central to the passage from von Allmen just quoted. I realize that the word may be problematic for readers of the free church traditions who speak of baptism and the Lord's Supper as ordinances rather than sacraments. While my understanding of the nature and effects of a sacrament may well go beyond what the free church tradition understands by an ordinance, I trust that my insistence on the necessity of faith (and thus of preaching) for the fruitful celebration of a sacrament will help to make my use of this word less problematic than it might otherwise be.

The close joining of word and sacrament, or, to use the fine phrase of von Allmen, "the preaching of the Word of God and the sacrament of the Word of God,"[4] is one of the recurrent emphases of the teaching of the Second Vatican Council. It is by the "preaching of the Word and the celebration of the sacraments" that missionary activity brings about the presence of Christ (Decree on the Church's Missionary Activity, #9). In local churches (dioceses) "the faithful are gathered together by the preaching of the gospel of Christ, and the mystery of the Lord's supper is celebrated, 'that by the flesh and blood of the Lord's body the whole brotherhood may be joined together' " (Dogmatic Constitution on the Church, #26). There are, as would be expected, several references to this interdependence of preaching and sacrament in the Constitution on the Sacred Liturgy. But where we find the relationship most clearly and explicitly developed is in the Decree on the Ministry and Life of Priests:

The People of God finds its unity first of all through the Word of the living God, which is quite properly sought from the lips of priests. Since no one can be saved who has not first believed, priests as co-workers with their bishops, have as their primary duty the proclamation of the gospel of God to all. . . .

Thus the ministry of the Word is carried out in many ways, according to the various needs of those who hear and the special gifts of those who preach. In areas or communities which are non-Christian, the gospel message draws men to faith and the sacraments of salvation. In the Christian community itself, especially among those who seem to understand or believe little of what they practice, the preaching of the Word is needed for the very administration of the sacraments. For these are sacraments of faith, and faith is born of the Word and nourished by it.

Such is especially true of the Liturgy of the Word during the celebration of Mass. In this celebration, the proclamation of the death and resurrection of the Lord is inseparably joined to the response of the people who hear, and to the very offering whereby Christ ratified the New Testament in His blood. The faithful share in this offering both by their prayers and by their recognition of the sacrament for what it is (#4).

It would be difficult to find a clearer statement of the Catholic position that the sacrament simply cannot exist without preaching, since there is no sacrament without faith and no faith without preaching. Obviously, this statement cannot be interpreted automatically to mean that there can be no celebration of a sacrament without a homily, for as the decree itself points out, "the ministry of the Word is carried out in many ways." Nonetheless, it is appropriate to the very nature of sacrament that its celebration be accompanied by the explicit preaching of the word of God, and in fact this is even seen to be required in those communities of Christians who seem to understand or believe little of what they practice. Finally, the appropriateness and indeed the necessity of preaching is especially to be noted in the celebration of the eucharist in which we find inseparably joined the proclamation of the death and resurrection of the Lord, the response of the people who hear, and the offering by which Christ confirmed the new covenant in his blood.

Thus the official teaching of contemporary Roman Catholicism holds there can be no sacrament without preaching precisely because there is no sacrament without faith, and faith comes from what is heard, and what is heard comes by the preaching of Christ (Rom. 10:17). It is precisely this emphasis which Catholics, with their long tradition of sacramental worship, need to hear. For most Protestant Christians the emphasis should probably be just the opposite: no preaching without sacrament. Once again this does not mean that every particular act of preaching must lead directly into a particular sacramental celebration. But it does mean, I believe, that the normal goal of preaching is either the sacrament of baptism in which, through word and gesture, the individual is incorporated into the church, that body of believers which is the body of Christ, or the sacrament of the Lord's Supper, in which the body of believers renews the covenant with the Father in the body and blood of Christ. And here too, I believe, this inseparable bond between preaching and the sacrament indicates that the weekly service in which Christians gather to remember and celebrate the victory of Christ over death is one in which preaching and sacrament will be the two essential components of their act of worship.

Worship, or liturgy, or sacrament, then, is something far more than the setting of the sermon. It is even more than the "*kairos*" of preaching, as one author put it, although there is no doubt that worship is the "opportune time when the word is preached in circumstances that allow its maximum efficacy."[5] It is, to use that old but at times still helpful category of scholastic philosophy, the "final cause" of preaching: its end, purpose, and goal. To say this is not to deny that preaching is to bring people to faith, or that it is to have an influence on their behavior. Rather, it is to affirm that faith and obedience are both to go one step further and be transformed into praise and thanksgiving. Unless this step is taken faith can all too easily degenerate into doctrinal rigidity, and obedience into legalistic conformity. Authentic praise and thanksgiving—that is, praise and thanksgiving flowing out of a recognition of the graciousness of God (faith) and propelling us to actions of love and justice (obedience)—is ultimately the mark of effective proclamation of the word of God.

Although the understanding of liturgy, and especially eucharistic liturgy, as the goal of preaching strikes me as the best way to understand the intimate connection between the two, it is not the only way of approaching the question. It is also possible, for instance, to interpret liturgy as a form of proclamation, and preaching as a form of worship. A case for the first approach is made by the authors of *Word and Table: A Basic Pattern of Sunday Worship for United Methodists*. There, the great thanksgiving prayer (also known as the eucharistic prayer) is described as a reflection of the very nature of Christianity in two ways: first of all, it is a "creedal act combining doxology and theology in a joyful statement of belief." Second, "the eucharistic prayer represents the whole biblical mentality of giving thanks by recital of what God has done."[6] Speaking of the eucharistic prayer as a statement of belief and as recital of the mighty acts of God is, in fact, saying that this prayer is proclamation, the telling forth of the good news of what God has done and is doing for his people.

A more usual way to speak of the interconnection between preaching and worship, however, seems to be in describing preaching as itself a form of worship. Fred Craddock writes that "the most, if not only, appropriate posture for the speaker is that of worship."[7] John Knox holds that preaching is not something that merely happens to be set in a context of worship or that proves most effective in that setting. "Rather, it cannot be really preaching except in that context. If the context of worship is not there already, the true sermon creates it. Either preaching contributes to, provides a medium of, worship, or it is not preaching at all."[8] And finally, Henry Mitchell refines this understanding of preaching as worship by speaking of it as celebration: "The best reinforcement and the greatest expression of joy must naturally occur when, so to speak, the lesson is completed and summarized, and thanks and celebration are offered for it at the end. All else leads us to this climactic moment, and whatever follows is inevitable anticlimax."[9]

To celebrate and offer thanks for the good news we have heard: that ultimately is the reason preaching and liturgy go together. We need to know why we should lift up our hearts. We need some reason to be able to answer the celebrant's "Let us give thanks to the Lord our God" with "It is right to give him thanks and praise." Why is it "right"? Why is God deserving of our thanks and praise? That is a question we can only answer out of faith, out of a vision and understanding of the way God is powerfully present in our world, in our lives. And we come to understand and believe in this power, presence, and promise through the word of those witnesses to his mighty acts in the past and through the word of those prophets who can discern his acts in the present. If that vision can be shared with us, if our faith can be inspired, deepened, bolstered, then we are enabled to lift up our hearts in praise and thanksgiving. In fact, we find that so doing is the fullest and most ennobling expression of all that it means to be human. Our lives are gathered together, given meaning, interpreted with a word that gives us a grandeur and dignity far surpassing the life of three score and ten which is the lot of ordinary mortals, much of it full of toil and trouble (Ps. 90:10).

And so we come again to the understanding of preaching that I hold to be central and essential: The interpretation of our concrete human situation by the word of God in such a way that people are led to turn to God in acts of praise and thanksgiving. The faith to which preaching invites people is the faith that God is actively and lovingly present in their lives, even when, to all appearances, this does not seem to be the case. In other words, it is preaching that proclaims the good news of the great and wonderful things God has done and is doing for his people, rather than preaching that lists the dos and don'ts that people must follow if they are to gain the favor of God. The preaching of good news is able to bring us to the recognition that we are loved, that our lives are meaningful, that sources of strength are available to us in this fellowship of faith and love which go beyond anything we might have hoped for. Such preaching helps us to see how, in the concrete situations of our lives, we are not caught up in some theater of the absurd, but rather that we are partners with God in a universe where the forces of truth, love, and justice that overcame sin and death in the person of Jesus Christ are now at work in the world in and through all who are joined with him in faith and baptism. This is the vision of life that the Christian preacher is called to share with all people, and in a special way with those followers of Christ who come together, week in and week out, to renew their hope in the kingdom which God is at work to establish and in which they believe they are called to share.

If such a case can be made for the close interdependence between preaching and the liturgy, why is this orientation to worship and sacrament so absent from contemporary preaching? Why, for instance, is it possible to read your way through the thirty-seven sermons contained in *The Twentieth Century Pulpit*,[10] a collection described on the jacket as a "powerful overview of twentieth-century preaching [which] contains representative sermons from men of diverse faith outlooks who have had a tremendous impact on the spiritual directions of our times" and find almost no reference to worship and little sense of a people gathered for prayer, praise, and thanksgiving? There are a couple of happy exceptions to this somewhat discouraging anthology of the best and the brightest—discouraging, at any rate, to one who looks for signs of a coming together again of preaching and liturgy. Edmund Steimle's sermon for All Saints' Day, "And How Does It All End?" is a marvelous call to rejoice in and give thanks for God's promise of resurrection, and to do so precisely at the time of year when everything around us seems to be dying. And Eduard Schweitzer's homily, "God's Inescapable Nearness," is a fine example of the verse-by-verse homiletic treatment of a text that takes seriously the fact that the people who are listening have come together for worship and that, in worship, God is near and in fact present. Carlyle Marney's "A Come and Go Affair" is explicitly preached as a communion sermon and calls the people to a real meeting with God. Ronald Knox's sermon, "The Window in the Wall," however, while it does deal with the eucharist, does so in reference to the service of benediction, a once popular devotion in which the consecrated host was venerated and used to impart a blessing to the people. The devotion grew out of a time when people took communion rarely and regarded the mass more as a propitiatory sacrifice than a covenant meal. The sermon is not at all representative of current Roman Catholic preaching or eucharistic theology and practice.

What is especially unfortunate in this collection of sermons is that there are so many in which an explicit reference to worship, especially eucharistic worship, would be a fitting compliment to the sermon's theme. For instance, D. M. Baillie's sermon, "The Doctrine of the Trinity," places great emphasis on God as continually present and active. This would seem to be a perfect place to speak of the special presence of God in liturgical and sacramental worship, but no such reference is made. Ernest T. Campbell in "No Faith, No Church," described as a keynote sermon for the season (Post Pentecost? Advent? Fall?), gives no indication that the church's new season begins with a eucharistic celebration. Reference to such a celebration would be germane to his point about faith being tied to the presence of Jesus, but the reference is not made.

Similar omissions of explicit references to worship can be noted in Harry Emerson Fosdick's "The Sacred and the Secular Are Inseparable" (there should be no difficulty in seeing how reference to the nature of sacramental worship would be appropriate in this context); in Gerald Kennedy's "Always in Debt," in which he shows how the recognition of our indebtedness is the ground of thanksgiving and joy; in Martin Luther King's "The Answer to a Perplexing Question" in which the concluding quotation from Revelation—"Behold I stand at the door and knock; if any man hear my voice, and open the door, I will come in to him, and will sup with him, and he with me"—provides the perfect lead into the eucharist; and finally Helmut Thielicke's "Journey without Luggage," whose point that when the crowds expect a word of judgment, God offers a promise rooted in the life of Jesus himself, provides a fitting motive for a response of praise and thanksgiving. But here again, as in all the other examples, the call is not made.

The impression one gets from these examples, therefore, is that preaching has very little indeed to do with worship. Worship may be a convenient place to preach, a nice occasion for it, a way of getting people settled down, a way of providing them with a "little extra," but in essence it would seem to be superfluous. The sermon can stand on its own. It is addressed to people's minds, and if something more than intellectual assent is intended, that something normally is to take place outside the church, in the "real world."

THE SPLIT BETWEEN PREACHING AND LITURGY

It is in this attitude toward liturgy as something unreal that we may find part of the answer to the question we posed earlier: Why this split between preaching and the liturgy when, from all we have seen, the two seem to be so naturally interdependent? Part of the blame may have to be laid at the feet of a liturgical expression that, in the early and high Middle Ages, became more and more divorced from the life of ordinary people and more and more the domain and responsibility of the professional clergy. All of us, Catholics and Protestants alike, are still reaping the results of a liturgy that over the centuries developed into a rite that became foreign to the people, not only in virtue of the language it used, but also because of a complicated or unfamiliar ritual that may have been rooted in the most mundane and necessary gestures but that gradually became arcane and esoteric. The response to this development was basically twofold: the Protestant rejection of abuses, which, although not intended to do away with the mass itself,[11] led to virtual elimination of the celebration of the eucharist as the normal Sunday community service, and the Catholic insistence on the efficacy of the rites in themselves, which, in effect, led to a minimalization of the importance of preaching in the life of the church.

A discomfortingly accurate picture of the way in which Roman Catholics of the not-too-distant past understood the relative importance of preaching and the sacraments is to be found in Edwin O'Connor's *Edge of Sadness*. The protagonist, Father Hugh Kennedy, muses on his own ministry of the word, and on the fact that Mr. Yee, who seems so attentive to his sermons, doesn't understand a word of English.

> And yet the saving thing is that it all couldn't matter less. The sermons, I mean. Granted that a good sermon is better than a bad one, what really counts—what *only* counts—is of course the Mass itself, and the people do come to that. As for the effectiveness or ineffectiveness of the sermon—well, who can measure these things? I know priests who are counted immensely successful in the pulpit: vibrant, eloquent men who capture a throng with a word. I don't for a moment doubt that they do

good work, but at the same time I always wonder how deep down the word really goes, and if it does go down, does it stay awhile, or is it gone overnight, like some bubble of a child's happy dream? One never knows. . . .[12]

The split between preaching and liturgy has had unfortunate consequences not only for the liturgy but for preaching as well. Preaching that fails to take advantage of the here-and-now characteristics of worship all too easily degenerates into abstract generalizations or historical reminiscing. The liturgy, understood and celebrated as the work of people gathered here and now for worship, demands that preachers address the here-and-now implications of the word of God for the life of the church.

So, what these final pages must attempt to do is indicate some ways in which this false split between preaching and liturgy can be overcome. Preaching that leads people to common work, to acts of praise and thanksgiving, is preaching that builds up a church. It gives the worshipers a sense of corporate identity and responsibility, enables them to recognize that they do not stand alone, that in their times of sorrow and joy they have someone to weep and rejoice with them, that they need not, as indeed they cannot, respond to the challenges of this world alone and unaided. Liturgical preaching brings about this sense of corporate identity by acting as a bridge between baptism and the eucharist. "When Baptism is not administered," writes Reginald Fuller, "it is the function of the liturgical sermon to reach back to the Baptism of the members of the congregation to renew in them the sense of membership of the ecclesia, and to lead forward to the liturgy of the Eucharist."[13]

The main concern of the remainder of this book will be with the eucharistic context of preaching, with some attention also devoted to the place of preaching in other sacramental and liturgical contexts, such as baptisms, weddings, and funerals. I recognize, of course, that for many Christians the eucharist is not the normal pattern of Sunday worship. I further recognize that the Roman Catholic pattern of eucharistic worship is the only one I know "from the inside." I hope, however, to speak out of my tradition and experience in such a way that my observations will have relevance for traditions and practices other than my own. Further, I trust that my admittedly limited familiarity with other traditions of worship through study as well as participation will enable me to be genuinely appreciative of and sympathetic toward non-Roman forms of worship and styles of prayer.

I do believe, however, that I should make two points quite explicit at this juncture. First of all, I believe that the eucharist is the central act of Christian worship and that it needs to become once again the regular and normative form of Sunday worship for all Christians. In other words, I do not believe that the Sunday service of the Lord's Supper can or should be understood as something peculiar to Roman Catholic tastes or preferences, a result of the strong sacramental emphasis of the Roman tradition. Gathering on the Lord's day to remember the Lord in the breaking of the bread is at the heart and origin of the Christian tradition, as is clear from the many studies that have been done in the area of liturgical history. It is also clear from Reformation studies that the principal leaders of the Protestant Reformation promoted the practice of the celebration of the eucharist on Sunday. However, as ironic as this may seem, the reason the practice did not last is that the people, accustomed as they were to receive communion only rarely, could not conceive of the possibility of communicating every Sunday. Thus, it was the medieval Roman Catholic eucharistic piety of excessive, almost superstitious reverence for the consecrated bread and wine that prevented Luther and Calvin, among others, from implementing their desire for a restoration of weekly communion to the Christian church. Monthly or even quarterly communion became the practice, with the normal Sunday service becoming a liturgy of the word.[14]

We see signs at present of gradual movement toward the Sunday eucharist as normative for all Christians. There are a number of reasons for this. For one thing, theological and liturgical studies on the nature of ritual action in general, and on the eucharistic ritual in particular, have helped Christians see this action not just as the reception of communion, or the offering of a sacrifice, but as a covenant meal in which they are called to participate. Also the restoration of the vernacular to Roman Catholic liturgical life has helped show that it is possible to combine a rich liturgy of the word with the sacramental celebration of the Lord's Supper in a weekly service which responds to the needs and abilities of contemporary men and women. Furthermore, scripture studies, by highlighting the importance of the meal in the overall ministry of Jesus, have helped us see that the eucharist is not to be understood as a mournful reenactment of that last meal that Jesus took with his disciples before he died. There is no doubt that the eucharist is a memorial of the last supper, but it also must be understood against the background of the multiplication of the loaves and the frequent occurrences of table fellowship between Jesus and his friends, both before and after his resurrection. At any rate, the Christ who is present to the believers in the breaking of the bread is not the dead Jesus hanging on the cross of Calvary or lying in the tomb, but the risen and victorious Savior, who invites us to his table in anticipation of the heavenly banquet, which he holds in readiness for all who follow him. When the eucharist is understood and administered (one could hardly say celebrated) as a memorial meal for a dead hero, it is no wonder that people are not eager to observe the ordinance more than a couple of times each year. When it is understood and celebrated as a regular gathering of the risen Lord with his friends, calling them to an ever deeper share in his new life, the weekly celebration becomes not only understandable but even necessary for the Christian disciple.

V. PREACHING AT THE EUCHARIST

The eucharist is at one and the same time memorial and celebration. It is celebration because what is being remembered is also being actualized. The kind of remembering that is at work in the eucharist is the kind that would be operative if we were to ask someone to remember us in their will (and we hardly need point out that the words "will," "testament," and "covenant" all overlap). In doing so, we certainly would have something more in mind than intellectual activity. We would be looking forward to a transfer of goods from that person to us. And that is exactly what is happening in the eucharist. We remember a God who remembers us, who is sharing his goods with us. We are in fact renewing, reaffirming the covenant God made with us in Christ, and this renewal is taking place through an act of remembering.

This action of remembering and renewing which is eucharist can be seen to be made up of three principal components or moments: the gathering of the people, the proclaiming of the law, and the renewal of the covenant.[1] Although preaching is most obviously and closely connected with the second stage, especially through the concern of the preacher to make clear the demands of the covenant law (the gospel) in the lives of people today, it also functions to gather the community through its repeated telling of the community's stories, and it leads the people forward to the renewal of the covenant.

THE GATHERING

Of these three major components of eucharistic worship, it is probably the first, gathering, that is receiving the most attention at the present time. While the gathering of the faithful used to be looked upon, when it was looked upon, as an obvious *sine qua non* before anything significant could happen, it is now being recognized as an event in its own right, a reality that cannot be presupposed or taken for granted, but that must be called into being again and again. Ultimately it is seen as *the* sign of the inbreaking of the kingdom of God, which will be perfected in the final gathering together of God's elect.

One finds signs of this renewed interest in and concern for the assembly almost everywhere one looks. For instance, the Fall 1979 issue of *Liturgy* has "Together Again" splashed across the front cover. Inside, Marianne Sawicki writes in Editor's Note:

> It's a together season of the year, and a time of together is dawning for the church. "Together again," we recall, is what Humpty Dumpty could not get. But it is the weekly privilege of each congregation to find itself "together again" when its members meet regularly as an assembly to worship. The Eucharist does for us the marvellous things that all the king's horses, etc., failed to accomplish for old Humpty. The "together again" experience, then, could be considered the paradigmatic experience of Christian worship. Moreover, that common weekly experience of the assembly has long been the ambition, the dream, the prayer of the ecumenically minded Christian Churches: *to get together again.*[2]

The gathering of the assembly is grounded in the reality of baptism, by which we are made into the body of Christ, joined to him as our head. It is because of this baptismal basis that liturgical preaching, according to von Allmen, is preaching that builds up rather than preaching that gathers in. In saying this, von Allmen goes on to warn against preaching in a way that "encourages an existential despair in which everything has constantly to be started afresh. . . . A Christian is not a brother of Sisyphus!"[3]

But while our baptism grounds us in a unity that is profound, it is a unity that is often not apparent because of cultural or social differences, or that is often weakened by human sinfulness, whether personal or inherited. For this reason there is a continuing need to gather the faithful, just as there is a continuing need to gather in those who do not know the Lord and have not accepted him through faith and baptism.

And so, we assemble. We come together as an identifiable group of people who, in spite of differences that may be profound and acute, share a common conviction that Jesus is central to the meaning and goal of human existence. The very fact that in this pluralistic world in which people are told they are free to go their own way, to do their own thing, to be themselves, we nonetheless come together to profess a common faith in the lordship of Jesus and perform a common action of offering thanks and sharing in a ritual meal is a remarkable phenomenon, becoming more and more remarkable as society gives evidence of becoming more and more fragmented. Because this assembling can no longer simply be accepted as a given, but must be seen as a freely chosen option, it is possible to see how important it has become, perhaps, as James White writes, "the most important single thing about worship."[4]

One of the functions of liturgical preaching, then, is to effect this gathering of the people of God, "to reach back to the Baptism of the members of the congregation, to renew in them the sense of membership of the ecclesia, and to lead forward to the liturgy of the Eucharist."[5] Obviously, it is not preaching alone that does this. It may be true that the singing of familiar hymns, the common recitation of prayers, especially when they are known by heart, or the seasonal repetition of ritual actions may be the most powerful and effective ways to gather a community and establish a sense of identity. But preaching has its role to play as well. And it will function best when the preacher is concerned not so much with saying something original as with a fresh, lively retelling of stories that are already familiar to people who have come together.

In referring to the familiar stories of the Christian community we are already at the heart of the liturgy of the word. But before beginning to speak of that part of the eucharistic liturgy in detail, it would be helpful to describe at greater length the particular elements that go into the rite of gathering.

It is a common practice for the leader of a Sunday morning service

to stand at the rear of the church after the service to greet the people
as they leave. Occasionally a significant encounter will take place
(for example, "I was really moved by what you said this morning, and
I wonder if I could stop in to see you sometime this week"). But
normally there is little more than the platitudinous "Nice sermon,"
or "Thank you for your message."

Would it not make more sense, I wonder, if the priest or minister
were to take up a position at the door of the church about twenty
minutes before the beginning of the service? People could be greeted
in a more leisurely way as they arrived (I imagine that the main
difficulty in such an arrangement would be the tendency of some
early arrivals to monopolize). While this would obviously not be the
time for lengthy or serious conversations, it is entirely possible that a
significant exchange could take place here as well, to be followed up
later in the week. But the main purpose of such a greeting and
meeting is that it helps to gather the community; it provides an
explicit form of welcoming to this time and this place for this
particular activity that we are about to do in common. There is no
doubt that such a welcome to the assembly can be provided by ushers
(or "ministers of hospitality" as they are more frequently called
nowadays), but this is not to imply that the presiding ministers are to
consider themselves excused from this service. It is part of their being
and function to represent the whole community, and their presence
at the door of the church can be a telling sign that the whole
community is welcoming and gathering together the individual
members of the congregation.

The greeting of the congregation before the service is also
beneficial in renewing the personal ties that bind minister and
congregation. When such a renewal of a pastoral relationship takes
place right before the service, leaders of worship are much less likely
to "officiate" (or, for that matter, to "preach"). Having revealed
themselves to their sisters and brothers as one with them in the
community of faith, they will be able to assume the role of leader and
preacher with the sense that they have been called forth by the
community, rather than imposed on it from above. Their presiding

and preaching will more easily have about it the character of service, rather than that of domination.

The greeting at the door by the leader of the worship service and/or the ministers of hospitality helps to make the transition from the world of eating and drinking, buying and selling, building and planting (see Luke 17:28) to the space and time specially set aside for corporate worship. Insist, as we must, that worship be in touch with people's lives, that it be worldly rather than escapist, we cannot pretend that the time we spend together for the Sunday eucharist is just like any other time together. There is a special character to this time and place, a special density or weightiness, and in order to enter into, or be gathered into, this privileged time and place, some kind of passage from the profane (*pro fanum*—before the temple) to the sacred must be provided for. True as it is that "liturgy is not a temple religion . . . it is the community gathered to do liturgy that is the special dwelling place of God," some assistance needs to be provided to enable this congregation to assemble not in some haphazard or informal way, but for the purpose of gathering "our total lives together before God, as a sacrifice of praise, with full consciousness and full awareness, with the kind of advertence that is unlikely or impossible in other—and partial—sectors of our lives."[6]

Obviously, for the community that comes together regularly every Sunday and that has a consciousness of what it is about, the ritual of gathering may be quite simple. It may in fact be little more than a period of quiet, with or without background music. It may even be possible, as the authors of *Word and Table* point out, that a short music rehearsal or an introduction to some new and unfamiliar element of the service can function as a ritual of gathering. As they go on to say, there is no one way that is necessarily better than another. Much depends on the nature and size of the congregation, the place that is being used, and, I might add, the relationship of the minister of worship to the congregation. If the minister is new or visiting, then it seems to me that there is a greater need for the minister to be personally involved in the ritual of gathering in order that the functions of presiding and preaching not be depersonalized.

However the rite of gathering is carried out, it is necessary that at some point there be a formal opening of the service, and that this opening take place on time. As for the nature of this formal beginning, I confess that my Roman Catholic background has led me to think almost instinctively in terms of greeting, that is to say, of some form of salutation by the leader of worship to the assembled congregation. I recognize now, however, that the solution is not so simple. The state of the question is well laid out by the Standing Commission of the Protestant Episcopal Church in the United States in a study document on the liturgy of the Lord's Supper. There they write of their difficulty resolving the question, How does one begin an act of corporate worship? The question concerns both the form of the beginning (an address to God or the address of officiant and congregation to one another) and the dominant attitude (one of adoration or unworthiness). From a slightly different point of view, one can speak of acclamation (alleluia, hosanna, Kyrie eleison), petition (Open our lips, Cleanse our hearts, Remember not our offenses), or bidding (The Lord be with you, Come let us worship).[7]

Although there may be no one correct solution, it is crucial that the celebrant begin the service in a formal way, preferably with one of the familiar and official formulas found in the rite that is being followed. This is not the time for "Good morning, everyone. Another beautiful day, isn't it? And wasn't that some game last night?" There is no denying that such chatter helps to establish rapport, puts some people at ease, and shows that you're OK. But the time for that is beforehand. This is the moment to shift gears, to begin in a formal way the action of praise and thanksgiving for which we have been gathered. To engage in chatter at this point, or even a "personal" good morning, complicates the movement from secular to sacred that is involved in all liturgical action.

The order of prayers, music, and acclamation that make up the opening moments of the community liturgy in the major Christian denominations is extremely varied. Rather than going into each of them in detail, it seems to me more important to warn against the danger of cluttering up this part of the service. One of the constants of liturgical history is that secondary rites and symbols tend to become inflated to the detriment of those which are primary. This tendency is especially noticeable in the entrance or gathering ritual of the eucharist. Hymn, greeting, exhortation, examination, confession, acclamation, and oration begin building on one another to such a degree that the reading of the word of God seems anticlimactic. It is important to remember the purpose of this rite of gathering—namely, to dispose a congregation for the attentive and receptive hearing of the word of God. If this is kept clearly in mind, then it is quite possible that on ordinary Sundays a vigorous opening hymn, a greeting, and a collect, this latter preceded by a generous period of silence, will be the most effective means of accomplishing this end.

However, it is possible to expand this opening rite, for the sake of added solemnity or for some other reason. There are various ways in which this can take place. For instance, following the hymn and/or greeting, it is possible for the leader of worship to introduce the theme of the day's liturgy. In some Roman Catholic circles, at least, the thematic approach to liturgical celebration has been so overdone that it is with some hesitation that I even use the word here. By "theme" I do not mean some idea or principle (e.g., social justice, family, brotherhood) in virtue of which scripture lessons have been chosen (or which has been forced out of the scripture lessons that are given) and, in general, around which the entire service has been structured. What I have in mind, rather, is a brief and pointed introduction to the liturgy of the day, with specific reference either to the particular feast that is being celebrated, or to the content of the lessons from scripture that will be read.

In the Roman Catholic liturgy a penitential rite is prescribed following the greeting. The sacramentary provides three forms and also indicates that this is one of the points in the liturgy when improvisation would be in order. Given some of the unhappy results, one is almost tempted to long for the days of rigid and inflexible rubrics! Far too often celebrants and liturgy planners have seized on the penitential rite as a place for exuberant and excessive creativity. What was designed as a brief moment to reflect on our unworthiness to come before the Lord, and then to acclaim the mercy of him who nonetheless invites us into his presence, has frequently become an occasion for a penitential fervorino followed by a particularized examination of conscience masquerading as a litany (For the times we have . . . , Lord have mercy).

Such an expansion of the penitential rite in Roman Catholic liturgical practice (and, I imagine, in other liturgical traditions as well) is problematic for a number of reasons. In the first place, it makes the entrance rite top heavy and cluttered. Second, there are some theological difficulties with the very placement of the rite for the confession of sin and assurance of pardon at this point in the liturgy of the eucharist, and these difficulties indicate that it should not be emphasized. One can certainly interpret the penitential rite at the beginning to mean that we do not come tripping lightly to an act of worship, but rather that we do so with a profound sense of our unworthiness. On the other hand, if we begin to think that we must somehow cleanse ourselves of our sins, and thus make ourselves worthy to come into God's presence, we are giving expression to a serious misunderstanding of the very heart of the gospel we preach, with its message of divine forgiveness and acceptance, with its insistence that our relationship with God is not grounded in anything we do, but rather in the fact that God loved us first, even when we were unworthy of that love.

Because of this understanding of the primacy of grace, there are liturgists who hold that it would be much more proper for the confession of sin and the assurance of pardon to conclude rather than introduce the liturgy of the word. It is the word of God that assures us of God's love, even while it points out our sins and allows us to admit to them, knowing that through the blood of Christ they have been forgiven. Such recognition of sin and assurance of pardon can be part of a special rite of penance following the homily, or perhaps incorporated into the general intercessory prayers. Or the homily itself can be the means of calling a congregation to repentance for its sin and offering it the continued assurance of God's love and pardon.

Obviously the call to confession is more appropriate during the penitential seasons of the year, namely Lent and to a lesser degree Advent. But even during these seasons liturgy planners and celebrants need to remember that the dominant theme of the penitential rite should be pardon and not introspection. "Kyrie eleison" is not so much the groveling plea of a wretched sinner, conscious of the depths of human depravity, as the faith-filled acclamation of the reborn sinner who remembers again God's tender mercy. For this reason, the litany of confession will more appropriately begin with the word "you" rather than "for" or "because" ("You are a God of love and pardon, Lord, have mercy" rather than "For the times we have been uncharitable, Lord, have mercy").

Normally the rite of gathering concludes with a collect, a short prayer said by the leader of worship which, in its classical form, is made up of four parts: address (O God . . .), motive (who . . .), petition (grant that . . .), and conclusion (through Christ our Lord). Whether this form is classically biblical or classically Roman (i.e., Latin) may be argued. Whatever the case, it seems to me that the appropriate form of prayer at this point in the service is one that is brief and pointed. The community has come together to hear the word of God and to celebrate the eucharist. We should get on with it.

PUBLIC READING OF THE SCRIPTURES

Does it still make any sense to include the public reading of the scriptures as a regular part of our worship? Could it not be argued that this act is simply blind traditionalism, a carryover from times and communities in which only a privileged few were literate? Would it not make more sense to provide everyone in the congregation with a Bible, announce the citation, and allow everyone to read the passage leisurely? Is it not conceivable that such personal reading of the text would allow for greater comprehension and retention than listening to it read, often poorly at that?

And yet, while recognizing that there may be a good deal of truth in such arguments, we continue to read the text. We do so, I believe, not simply out of some unthinking adherence to tradition, but because of a deep-seated conviction that it is only when a text is read aloud and heard that it achieves its full power to communicate on the levels of both intellect and emotion. This is not to say that a text read privately cannot move us. I imagine that everyone, at one time or another, has had the experience of being completely transported, either to joy or sorrow, while reading, or of being drawn into such close communion with an author by means of the written word that you felt the author were sitting beside you.

But what if you had the chance to hear an author like Flannery O'Connor read one of her stories? Is it not altogether likely that you would discover a level of meaning, an immediacy of address that is not accessible to you when you read it in the privacy of your room? She herself seemed to think that such a deeper level of communication was possible, and especially so when the people who heard her read her stories had some familiarity with the people and situations she was writing about. In a letter to a friend she remarks: "Last Wednesday I went to the University of Georgia and read that night 'A Good Man Is Hard to Find.' It was a perfect audience because they caught everything, it all being familiar to them."[8] Is it not altogether possible that something of this increased level of understanding and enjoyment would come through even if you were to hear the story read by someone else, someone who knew her work well and was skilled in the art of oral interpretation? And, further, if you were to hear this story read in the company of other listeners, would not the fact of your participating in this common experience out of your own shared experiences intensify the meaning of the story for you? In the same letter, Flannery O'Connor mentions that when she reached the point where Red Sammy Butts comes in, "there was an appreciable titter of another order that *rolled through* the audience. . . . Later somebody told me that the character of Red Sammy was not unlike the character of Wally [Butts, University of Georgia football coach]."[9]

What, in principle, would be true of the works of an author like O'Connor is even more true of the texts of the Bible since, for the most part, they originated as a spoken rather than a written word. The stories of the patriarchs and kings, the exhortations and diatribes of the prophets, the admonitions of wise men, the prayers of the psalmist, and, of course, the sayings of Jesus all find their origin in the spoken word. And even in the epistolary sections of the New

Testament we find indications that they were written to be read aloud: "And when this letter has been read among you, have it read also in the church of the Laodiceans" (Col. 4:16).

Thus, the reason that the scriptures continue to be read in the liturgical assembly is that their meaning and power may be intensified and that their author (ultimately, as we believe, God himself) be made more present. This latter purpose is emphasized in the Constitution on the Liturgy: "Christ is present in His Word, since it is He Himself who speaks when the Holy Scriptures are read in the church" (#7). "In the liturgy God speaks to his people and Christ is still proclaiming his Gospel" (#33).

In each of these statements of the council we can detect a conscious effort to emphasize the importance of the public reading of the scriptures. Paragraph 7 of the constitution, from which the first quotation is taken, is drawn for the most part from Pope Pius XII's 1947 encyclical letter on the liturgy, *Mediator Dei*. In that document Pius speaks of the presence of Christ at mass in the person of the minister and in the eucharistic elements, but he makes no mention of the presence of Christ in the reading of the scriptures. That was explicitly added by the framers of the constitution, over the objections of some of the council fathers. In answer to their objections the conciliar commission responded: "In the liturgical tradition, however, Christ is said to speak when the Scriptures are read; nay more, the presence of Christ in the Gospel is celebrated, especially in the Eastern liturgies" (Murray, "The People and the Book," p. 393).

It is thus apparent, as one commentator on the constitution put it, that we are dealing with something more than a vague and inert "symbolic" presence. The presence of Christ in the reading of the scriptures is an active and personal presence.[10] In fact, one can speak of the "real presence" of Christ in the reading of the scriptures in much the same way that some Christian traditions speak of Christ's real presence in holy communion.

We can then say that the reading of the scriptures in the liturgical assembly is sacramental in that it is an effective sign of the presence of Christ. This being the case, not only should the reading of the scriptures not be omitted, as for example, Billy Graham does at the beginning of his sermon on the Prodigal Son ("Now tonight, let's turn to the 15th chapter of Luke. I'm not going to read the passage because it's too long . . ."[11]), but everything should be done to ensure that the reading is performed with care and intelligence. This is especially true when the person who preaches is also the reader of the text. A slovenly or hurried reading is a clear sign of the preacher's disregard for the words of scripture no matter how strong the sermon's avowals of reverence may be. And in those cases when the reading of the lesson is done by someone other than the preacher, the preacher will want to ensure that the lector is properly trained for this important ministry. In his Rule for Monasteries, Benedict wisely writes that public reading is not to be left to anyone who happens to pick up the book. Unfortunately, that is all too often what happens in some parish communities. We seem to operate on the assumption that since everyone can read, anyone can read publicly. We regard public reading as little more than the semiautomatic translation of visual symbols into vocal symbols, forgetting that those visual symbols have to pass through mind and heart and be shaped by them if the spoken word is to communicate the emotional color and intellectual content that the author tried to capture and disseminate through the written word.

If Christ is present when the holy scriptures are read in church, he is present to the degree that those scriptures are read well. And for that to happen, training in the skill of oral interpretation is a necessity for virtually everyone. Like every other skill, the skill of reading well in public is acquired through practice, as well as through a knowledge of the theory that undergirds it. In large measure the generally accepted theories and techniques of oral interpretation are applicable to the reading of scriptural texts. In addition there are, I believe, some principles and points of practice specific to the reading of scripture in a liturgical setting that should be mentioned.

In the first place, it is essential to remember that the "through faith to faith" principle (see Rom. 1:17) applies as much to the reading of the texts of scripture as to the preaching that flows from those texts. We read not to entertain or even to inform, but to communicate faith to one another. The liturgical reading of scripture is not performance so much as ministry—service to Christ and to the community. It is therefore essential that the reader believe what is read. Absolutely nothing can compensate for this, for the reader who would stand to proclaim a text while not believing in it would be engaging in hypocrisy and would jeopardize the profoundest meaning of the text. However, to believe what we read does not imply that we must be literalists in our interpretation of the text, resolutely banishing every doubt and difficulty as a sign of lack of faith. What believing does imply is a willingness to hear God speaking to his people through the words we read, calling them away from their slavery to sin and to freedom.

In the actual carrying out of their ministry, readers should be careful to distinguish the liturgical introductions and conclusions of the text from the text itself. This can best be done if the reader looks at the congregation while saying "A reading from the Letter of Paul to the Galatians" (or whatever the introduction is) and then pauses for a good three to five seconds before beginning the actual reading. Likewise, in those traditions in which a liturgical formula calling for a response from the people is appended to the reading, it is important for the reader to pause at the end of the reading, look at the congregation, say "This is the word of the Lord" (or the equivalent formula) and then *remain looking* at the congregation until the response has been given. Most readers find this almost impossible to do. They say the concluding formula and immediately look down to the book, or even begin to move away from the lectern. Such behavior is a subtle but effective indication to the congregation that they are little more than passive recipients who have no essential role to play in the act of worship. On the other hand, the reader who waits on the response of the congregation indicates that active listening is a form of liturgical participation, and that the word of God becomes actively and fully present when intelligent reading and active listening are joined.

The lectionary provides for a psalm response following the Old Testament reading. Ideally, this response should be sung, the antiphon being taken by the congregation and the verses by a chanter or choir. When this is not possible, it is important that the psalm not be read in the same way as the lesson. There should be a significant break between the lesson and the psalm (at least ten seconds) and, if at all possible, the psalm should be led by someone other than the reader, the better to indicate the function of the psalm as the people's response to the reading.

Liturgical rites have generally accorded greater honor to the reading of the gospel than to the other scriptures. The reading is assigned to a deacon, if one is serving the parish, and is preceded by special prayers and blessings. On very solemn occasions the gospel book is carried in procession to the lectern, and is accompanied by candles and incense. The people stand as the gospel is proclaimed, a tradition that can be traced back to the third-century canons of Addai: "At the conclusion of all the scriptures, let the Gospel be read, as the seal of all the scriptures, and let the people listen to it standing upon their feet, because it is the glad tidings of salvation to all men," and finally the book is kissed at the end of the reading.

Christians who come from a tradition that emphasizes simplicity and straightforwardness may find such marks of honor excessive, and may rightly point out that the word of God to which we are to give reverence is not a book, but the word of God preached and heard. I am in accord with this view, and for that reason find that the lifting up of the book at the words "This is the gospel of the Lord" is a misdirecting of attention to the book rather than to the word proclaimed and preached. On the other hand, it does seem entirely appropriate that the appearance of the book and our reverent handling of it give visual expression to our faith that in and through this written record the word of God is made available to us. There can certainly be no justification for reading the scriptures from a tattered and dog-eared leaflet that is then tossed aside, or from a limp paperback Bible out of which all manner of improvised bookmarks are protruding. One may dispense with the candles and the kissing, but one should not dispense with a decent, indeed handsome book. It may even be possible to create a special binding for the gospel book so that it can be a thing of beauty. One author describes how this was done by making use of the silver and gold removed from the old chalices, patens, and other liturgical vessels that were no longer being used. The end result, he remarks, was a rather heavy book, but, he adds, the word of God is a weighty matter.[12]

THE HOMILY

It has been the main thesis of this book that the homily is an integral part of the liturgical action in which the words of scripture are used to interpret the lives of the people in such a way that they are enabled to participate in the liturgical action with faith. Since the homily is to flow out of the particular scriptures that have been read, von Allmen insists that one gesture should be absolutely forbidden: "that of shutting the Bible after reading the text of the sermon and banishing it to the edge of the pulpit."[13] The open Bible or lectionary is a telling sign of the preacher's desire to hand on that which is received (see I Cor. 15:1).

What of the nature of the homily itself? Does it have any set form, any particular style by which it can be identified as a specific kind of public address? Is there an ideal length?

I do not think it is possible to give a particular and definite response to each of these questions. The reason for this is that what is specific to the homily is not its content (scriptural), or even its form, but its function. It is, as John Burke would say, "function-indicating, not content-determining."[14] However, I do think it can be said that the style most appropriate to the homily is the style of personal address. Donald Macleod notes that "homily" is derived from the Greek words *omou* (together) and *ile* (a crowd). "*Homilia* was an assembly, and the connotation of the word had to do with 'communicating with a crowd.' "[15] One of its earliest appearances, he says, was Acts 20:11, which he translates, "And [Paul] had broken bread and *talked* a long while."

But while speaking to a crowd may be implied in the etymology of the word, the actual use of the verb *homileo* in the New Testament indicates that the form of address was much more conversational than that employed by the classical Greek orator. The word is used in reference to the conversation the two disciples engaged in as they were on their way to Emmaus "talking [homiloun] with each other about all the things that had happened" (Luke 24:14). The word is also used for the conversation that Antonius Felix, procurator of Judea, had with Paul when the latter was held prisoner in Caesarea: "He sent for him often and conversed [homilei] with him" (Acts 24:26). We may therefore imagine that Paul's talk with the congregation at Troas was really more of a conversation than a sermon, and in fact the RSV translation of Acts 20:11 reads: "he conversed with them a long while."

Thus, if the etymology of the word homilia implies speaking to a crowd, the way the verb homileo is actually used in the New Testament would seem to imply that this crowd is not some haphazard conglomerate of anonymous strangers, but a gathering of friends, people with whom one is familiar and to whom one can speak comfortably and easily. In fact, we might even go so far as to say that the expression "dialogue homily" is, in a sense, redundant, since the homily is by its nature dialogic in principle if not in method.[16]

While the mode of communication of the homily may be comfortable and easy, its content is of ultimate concern. Ease and comfort, therefore, must not be interpreted to mean that homilies can be thought of as a few folksy reflections on the scriptural passages which can be thrown together a few minutes before the service. I trust that my earlier description of a method for moving from the scriptural text to preaching leaves no doubt that an effective homily, that is, one that helps people to interpret their lives in such a way that they are enabled to come before God with praise and thanksgiving, demands of the preacher ample time and hard work. My point here is that the results of this creative work should be offered to the congregation in such a way that the homily sounds more like one person speaking to another about something that really matters, than like a lecture delivered by a professor before a class.

How can this be done? How can we prepare a homily so that when we actually do stand before a congregation to preach, our words have about them something of the immediacy and personal quality that seems to come so naturally when we are conversing with friends?

One way to do this is to write out the homily (to say that a homily should be written is not to say that it should be read) as if you were writing a letter to a friend. What we usually do when we begin to draw together our ideas for a homily and put them on paper is fall into the term paper or essay genre of writing. The model of the research paper or critical essay, which we spent so many of our school years trying to perfect, is a hard one to shake; it is only by consciously adopting another model that we will be able to put personal feeling, personal interest, and personal conviction into our preaching.

This conversational approach to preaching is certainly not something new. It may appear to be so, because it is difficult to provide written models of such preaching for study. Conversations do not print up well; essays and formal discourses do. And yet, we can find evidence of this more familiar form of address in the preaching of some of the early church fathers: the baptismal catecheses of Cyril of Jerusalem, for example, or the homilies on the Psalms or on the Gospel of John of Augustine. And much closer to our time, but still in an age that seems so remote, homiletically speaking at least, there were those who pleaded for a less formal style of discourse in preaching. The advice to write a sermon as if one were writing a letter, for example, comes from an 1895 lecture on preaching by one W. Body Carpenter. In that lecture he goes on to tell the preacher:

> Try and realize that your object is to persuade, to instruct, to help, and to edify. You are not writing for a professor's eye; there is no prize at stake, except this—the prize of being able to help some anxious, sorrowful, or perplexed heart. Let your wish be to say what you have to say so that it may bring food to the hungry heart, and you will surely fall into a natural and unaffected style of address.[17]

This "natural and unaffected style of address" will also be enhanced to the degree that the preacher remains close to the text of the lesson(s) and allows the structure of the homily to be determined by the flow of the text itself. To do so, comments one author, "will provide a meditative and conversational style rather than an argumentative and reasoned style; an intimate devotion rather than a proclamatory and heraldic stance."[18]

What about the length of the homily? While there can be little doubt that the mass media have conditioned us to receive information in short, quick-paced spots, I do not think we can automatically conclude that the only kind of preaching that will be effective is the three- to five-minute homily. The reason many people find preaching intolerable, I believe, is not simply because it is too long. The reason is that they find it unbearably banal, addressing no significant issue or idea. And when you are forced to listen to someone who says nothing, then even two minutes can seem like an eternity. In short, long homilies are homilies that seem long; short homilies are homilies that seem short. The time by which we measure preaching is not so much clock time (*chronos* in the Greek) as felt time (*kairos*). When we are engaged in an important and personally involving communication with someone, we lose consciousness of time. Clock time flies; felt time stands still.

And yet, we have to deal with the realities of schedules and people's expectations. A congregation expects a normal Sunday service to last about one hour, and if this service is to include the eucharist, then it is simply not going to be possible to preach for a half hour or more. To reduce the length of time allotted to preaching, however, does not necessarily imply that its importance is being minimized. As the authors of *Word and Table* rightly point out, "Preaching may gain in strength by being shortened and sharply focused."

It is surely no secret that a good bit of time in many of the traditional half-hour sermons is taken up by exegetical detail (absolutely necessary in the study but not in the pulpit), clever but irrelevant anecdotes, "filler" quotations, and theological argument that may be more of a reflection of seminary memories than of attempts to deal with current concerns. If some of this padding were to be removed, an attempt made to identify a specific human concern to which the word of God could be addressed, and the homily clearly structured and thought through, there seems to be no reason why the preacher would not regularly be able to preach a homily of ten or fifteen minutes. This length of time would seem to be about right for an hour's service, for then the liturgy of the word and the liturgy of the eucharist would take about the same amount of time. Von Allmen notes that a short sermon (which, for him, means one fifteen to twenty minutes long) can be justified if communion is to be celebrated. "The table standing prepared dispenses us from a long sermon," he writes, "because its aim is similar to that of the sermon: namely, to permit a living contact (with the mutual gifts which such a contact implies) between Jesus and the Church."[19]

The emphasis of recent liturgical theology on the unity of the liturgy of word and eucharist should clearly indicate that normally the preacher of the homily and the presiding minister of the eucharist will be one and the same person. In those cases when a guest preacher is present, the arrangement of the service should be such that it is clear that the person who presides at the eucharist also presides at the word, and that it is at the presiding minister's invitation that the preacher is called forward.

In the Roman Catholic Church at the present time, only priests and deacons can be officially licensed to preach at the eucharist, although the practice of nonordained men and women preaching a liturgical homily is not uncommon in some communities. What may be emerging in the Catholic Church is an understanding that the ordained clergy's responsibility for the preaching of the word may mean that they are responsible for ensuring that the word of God be preached, either by themselves or by those gifted members of the community who may be called forth. Such a development should be encouraged, I believe, for it provides a way of combining a charismatic approach to preaching (that is, a recognition that the ability to preach is a gift that can be freely given to anyone) with the recognition that preaching needs "ordering" if it is to be a faithful witness to the gospel.[20]

While there may still exist in the Catholic Church serious objection to lay preaching in the liturgy of the eucharist, there is very little objection to a quite common practice that strikes me as a liturgical abuse. I speak of the custom in some large communities of having one priest or deacon preach at all the Sunday masses, including those at which another priest presides. The justification given for such a practice is that the quality of preaching is improved when a person does not have to preach every week. This may be true, although by no means evident, but because of the division this practice sets up between the liturgy of the word and the liturgy of the eucharist, it is a custom that I believe needs serious reconsideration. If the practice is to continue, then I think the least that should be demanded of the preacher is that he be present for and participate in the entire liturgy. His popping in to read the gospel, and then popping out again after the homily, is hardly calculated to support an understanding of the homily as an integral element of the eucharistic liturgy. Besides, it's just bad manners.

THE LITURGY OF THE EUCHARIST

It is quite possible that a liturgical homily could be preached without any explicit reference to the liturgical action itself. The purpose of the homily is to prepare people to celebrate the liturgy, and if, after having heard a homily at the celebration of the Lord's Supper, the people are ready to make eucharist, that is, praise and thank the Father for the way in which he has blessed their lives through Jesus Christ, and to receive from him the body and blood of his Son as the pledge of his continuing covenant with us, then the homily has accomplished its purpose even though the words "communion," "eucharist," "Lord's Supper," or "mass" may never have been uttered.

Normally, however, a specific reference to the sacrament to be celebrated, whether this be briefly noted or developed at some length, is to be expected in the liturgical homily. And such a reference need not always come at the end, although it does seem to come most naturally there as a lead-in to the sacramental action that follows. The regular omission of any reference to the liturgy we are celebrating makes about as much sense as the omission in an after-dinner speech of any reference to the reason people have come together, or the omission in a talk given at a pep-rally of any remarks about the forthcoming game. If people come together to make eucharist, the word addressed to them should have something to do with the "why" and "how" of giving thanks; if the service is one of reconciliation, then the word of scripture should be used to address the "why" and "how" of being reconciled. The frequent, almost regular, omission of such references in liturgical preaching, especially at the eucharist, is undoubtedly one of the reasons the homily, even when based on the texts of the day, seems to be a foreign element in the liturgical service rather than an integral part of it.

THE RITE OF PREPARATION

When the homily is understood as a functional word enabling the gathered community to respond with praise and thanksgiving to God, it makes sense to move rather directly from the homily to the eucharistic prayer. Occasionally a pause for reflection after the homily may be in order, but when this becomes a regular feature of the liturgy, the homily once again takes on the character of an independent, almost isolated unit within the total liturgical action.

In the communion rites of several denominations the recitation or singing of the Nicene Creed is prescribed after the homily on Sunday. While a case can be made for the appropriateness of the homily's serving to lead a congregation to a common profession of its faith by means of a classical and ancient formulation, there is a certain *embarras des richesses* in calling for the recitation of this creedal statement at each Sunday eucharist. The eucharistic prayer is itself a statement of faith, "combining doxology and theology in a joyful statement of belief."[21] For this reason an additional creedal statement was looked upon as redundant by much of Western Christianity during most of its history.

Following the recitation of the creed, provision is made for the general intercessory prayers or prayers of the faithful. The inclusion of this prayer in reformed eucharistic rites is not only a restoration of the earliest pattern of eucharistic worship,[22] but also provides a fitting response to the word preached. Having received again the message of a kind and loving Father, we bring before him the needs of the church, the whole world, and of our community, and then proceed to offer him our prayers of praise and thanksgiving. It should hardly be necessary to say that the formulation of these petitions, if they are not to be spontaneously made by the congregation, should be made by the preacher in the light of what was said in the homily. However, care should be taken to maintain the universal or general character of this prayer, not allowing it to become overly particularized in reference to the homily or the needs of a specific community.

Then follows the presentation or preparation of the gifts of bread and wine. Although these rites are generally quite simple, we again find a tendency to inflate the secondary elements of the liturgy. For example, in the present rite for the preparation of the gifts in the Roman eucharist, the prayers and ritual actions presently prescribed are much more elaborate than those which were proposed in the "*missa normativa*," the reformed eucharistic rite drawn up by the Consilium to implement the Constitution on the Liturgy. They represent, writes Frederick R. McManus, a kind of "liturgical backsliding."[23]

While we may all live and pray with traditions of worship that are less than perfect, it is important to have an educated understanding of the structure of the rites that we have inherited, and to make prudential judgments on the basis of this understanding. If the rites of presentation and preparation are less important than the preaching of the word and the proclamation of the great prayer of thanksgiving, we should take care that we not contribute to their further inflation. Thus, for example, Roman Catholics and others who have adopted the practice may need to look critically at the appropriateness of emphasizing the offertory procession, especially when such a procession consists of little more than bringing to the front of the church bread and wine, which the celebrant or someone else had carried to the back of the church before the service began. If there are prayers to accompany the preparation of the gifts, it is better to say these prayers quietly and unobtrusively. If, as in the Lutheran tradition, the singing of the hymn of the day customarily follows the sermon, it may be necessary to take care lest the singing of this hymn assume such importance that it overshadow the eucharistic prayer as the response of the congregation. In Germany, notes Fuller, the singing of the chorale was so emphasized that the liturgical tradition "became in the end little more than a recitation of the words of institution as a prelude to communion. The people, having received the Word in the sermon, and having responded to that Word in the chorale, receive the sacrament as a confirmatory appendage to the sermon."[24]

Finally, some churches may need to look again at the way in which they highlight the presentation of the people's monetary offerings. While it is certainly true that "the offering is more than money; it is the symbolic offering to God of ourselves and all that we have,"[25] care should be taken that this offering of our gifts to God not be ritualized in such a way that it begins to appear that what we do for God is more important than what he does for us, or that it is in our financial wealth that we have the most solid assurance of God's love for us. A simple bringing forward of the people's offerings (and there is no reason why the clergy should not contribute to the collection as well as the laity), and their reception by the presiding minister along with the bread and the wine to be used in the sacrament, would seem to be sufficient.

THE EUCHARISTIC PRAYER

It is in the great prayer of thanksgiving that the Sunday service reaches its highpoint. At least this is the way it should be. In actuality, however, the prayer comes across most often as something of a letdown. One of the principal reasons for this is that the eucharistic prayer frequently is characterized by all the worst features of monologue: a familiar, fixed text recited without feeling by one person before a passive assembly of reluctant churchgoers.

The fact that in some traditions the text (or texts) of the eucharistic prayer is fixed is not in itself an insurmountable problem (think, for example, of the Lord's prayer). What is more problematic is the practice of having one person pray this text aloud in the name of the entire worshiping community. Unless such texts are of high poetic quality, they do not bear up under continued repetition.[26] Instead of uniting the worshipers into an ever deepened union with the mystery

of death and life that is being celebrated, they alienate those who
hear them because their language is so commonplace.

There would seem to be two solutions to the present difficulty:
provision for more officially approved texts in churches where the
eucharistic prayer is not left to the improvisation of the celebrant,
and/or the acceptance of improvisation. [27]

Celebrants who are able to improvise, or at least adapt, the
eucharistic prayer are in an especially advantageous position.
Obviously such improvisation should not be attempted without a
clear understanding of the structure of this kind of prayer. As a
beginning, one could check the outline presented in *Word and
Table* (pages 44-46). Provided one has a good sense of the elements of
such prayer and their relationship to one another, and, even more
important, provided one has been formed by close familiarity with
classic formulations, dignified and theologically sound eucharistic
prayers are not that difficult to compose. And because such
compositions or adaptations provide for the possibility of making
explicit references to the particular signs of God's love that were
highlighted in the lessons and homily, such original or adapted
eucharistic prayers become the most ideal way of drawing the liturgy
of the word and the liturgy of the eucharist into a unified expression
of faith and worship.

But what of those traditions in which the text or texts of the
eucharistic prayer are fixed? Although it may not be possible for
celebrants to alter the text of the prayer so that it includes specific
allusions to the good news that was proclaimed on a particular day,
they may still give expression to the unity of the liturgy of the word
and the liturgy of the eucharist by alluding to or making use of a
phrase from the eucharistic liturgy in their homily. What is of
greatest importance, however, is that the celebrant pray these texts
with a sense of conviction. They must not be seen simply as formulas
to be gotten through, but as a set way in which the church gives
expression to its belief in and response to its God. To draw on the
advice that Benedict gives his monks with regard to the praying of the
psalms, the celebrant must pray the great thanksgiving in such a way
that the mind is in harmony with the voice. [28] Only in such a way will

the congregation have the sense that their corporate prayer is being gathered together in one great act of thanksgiving.

The rites surrounding the communion and the dismissal will provide further opportunities for a word from the celebrant that will help focus the celebration in the light of what has been said in the homily. However, a word of caution should be repeated. Attempts to give unity to a celebration can easily be overdone. It is not necessary that every hymn, every reading, every prayer, and every visual component of the celebration be directly tied into some specific overarching theme. To do so can easily make the liturgy a head trip, more of an intellectual exercise than a common act of worship. We need to remember that we are celebrating not some idea but an event, God's outpouring of his love for us in the death and resurrection of Jesus and the abiding presence of his Spirit in the community of believers. We may want to focus on one or the other expression of that love, but what we always come back to is not a theme but a person, the risen Christ, in whom the fullness of God is revealed and through whom he sends his life-giving Spirit into the world.

VI. PREACHING AT
BAPTISMS, WEDDINGS, AND FUNERALS

Generally, liturgical preaching is understood as preaching at the celebration of the eucharist. There is no doubt that this is where most liturgical preaching takes place. However, given our renewed awareness that the ordinances or sacraments of the church are signs of faith, that faith comes through hearing, and that even within the Christian community faith needs constantly to be reawakened, we are coming to the realization that each coming together of the Christian community for prayer, for a service of initiation, blessing, commissioning, or comfort, is a response to the invitation God offers us in his word.

The celebration of baptism, the preeminent sign of faith, which, along with the eucharist, is accepted by all Christians as an evangelical sacrament or ordinance, is a privileged time for the gospel to be preached with power and gladness. Ideally, such preaching will not be confined to the actual service in which baptism is celebrated, but will extend over an indefinite period of catechesis during which the rites preparatory to baptism are carried out.

In the Roman Catholic Church the restoration of the rite for the Christian initiation of adults is helping to call attention to the special baptismal emphasis in the Sundays of Lent, and, in fact, to the whole season of Lent as a time during which catechumens receive their final preparation for the sacrament of baptism and the entire Christian community is prepared to renew its baptismal commitment at the Easter vigil. This baptismal emphasis is especially to be found in the third, fourth, and fifth Sundays of Lent. It was on these Sundays that the "scrutiny" of the catechumens took place, not so much a final examination of the candidates' readiness for baptism (they were "elected" for that on the first Sunday of Lent) as a powerful summing up for them of the meaning of this sacrament. At the liturgy of the word on these three Sundays, the key texts were taken from the Gospel of John: the meeting between Jesus and the Samaritan woman at the well (chapter 4); the curing of the man born blind (chapter 9); and the raising of Lazarus (chapter 11). The obvious intent of these choices was to complete their baptismal catechesis by presenting Christ as living water, as light, and as life.

This order of readings from the Gospel of John has been preserved in the lectionary for the Sundays of the A cycle (with some slight alteration in the Lutheran lectionary). However, in the introduction to the Roman Catholic lectionary we read, "Since these passages are very important in relation to Christian initiation, they may also be used for years B and C, especially when candidates for baptism are present" (#13).

Even though other gospel texts are provided for years B and C (the introduction notes that "for pastoral reasons, many wished another choice of texts"), a good argument can be made, I believe, for using the year A cycle every year. In the first place, every effort should be made to arrange schedules and programs in such a way that adult candidates for baptism are fully initiated into the faith on the feast of feasts when the church celebrates Christ's victory over sin and death, a victory that becomes ours through faith and baptism. In those churches where infant baptism is practiced, it should also be possible, provided intelligent explanations are given and the alternative is presented in as attractive a manner as possible, that all children born just before and during Lent be baptized at Easter. And finally, even in those communities where the baptismal font is barren at Easter, the renewal of baptismal promises, which is, or should be, central to our celebration of Easter, indicates that our preaching during the time of Lent be directed to this end.

Frankly, it is difficult to see what kind of serious "pastoral reasons" could have prompted the provision of alternate texts for years B and C. The Johannine accounts of Jesus and the Samaritan woman, the cure of the man born blind, and the raising of Lazarus are of such profundity that yearly repetition at the Sunday eucharist would only increase rather than lessen our appreciation of their literary, theological, and spiritual richness. They are, it seems to me, the kind of texts that preachers and people would look forward to each year as they prepare to celebrate the resurrection of Christ and their sharing in that new life through baptism.

If adult candidates for baptism are present in the congregation during the season of Lent, the preacher will speak to them of the dignity, promise, and demands of the Christian calling in such a way that the preaching can be "overheard" by the entire congregation and provide them with the opportunity to reflect on their own Christian calling and thus be readied to recommit themselves to it in a formal way at the great Easter liturgy. This indirect form of preaching is described in detail by Fred Craddock in his book, *Overhearing the Gospel*. Preaching to candidates for baptism would seem to be one of the natural ways to implement the method he outlines.

Such preaching to be overheard can also be done at the regular Sunday eucharistic service at which baptism will take place. The scripture lessons read on those occasions should be those of the Sunday, and not special lessons chosen in view of the celebration of baptism. In preparing the homily the preacher might look to the lessons for an indication of just what it is God offers us through baptism. The homily can then be preached in such a way that the congregation is called to an awareness of its baptismal dignity and its responsibility to share that gift with the neophytes, and in fact with the whole world.

WEDDINGS

The purpose of preaching at a wedding is not to relate personal anecdotes about the couple's courtship, to offer them helpful hints for a happy married life, to present a theology of marriage and the family, or (God forbid, but it does happen) to condemn the evils of divorce, birth control, and/or abortion. Rather, the gospel is preached to enable husband and wife to give themselves fully to each other in love and to call them and the witnessing congregation to celebrate that love as a sign of God's continuing presence in his church.

The preparation for the marriage ceremony affords the preacher an ideal opportunity for involving the hearers of the word in the formulation of the homily. Even in those cases when a couple asks for "the traditional wedding," they can still be asked to choose the texts of scripture that they wish to have read. A list of appropriate texts, or an actual booklet containing these texts, should be provided them to help in the choice. This request should be made early enough so that they can indicate their choice, and the reasons for the choice, to the minister well before the ceremony. In almost all cases preachers will find that their conversations with the engaged couple will provide them with the germinal idea for a homily that will be both scriptural and personal.

In these planning sessions preachers and pastors will on occasion find that a couple will propose one or more nonscriptural readings for the service—a sonnet of Shakespeare or the chapter on marriage from Khalil Gibran's *Prophet*, for instance. In such situations it may help to explain that the reason texts from the Bible are read at a wedding is not simply because they have some good or beautiful things to say about love and marriage, but because they are the means by which we remember the Lord in whom this marriage is being celebrated. Nonscriptural readings (or purely secular music, for that matter) that may be especially meaningful to the couple would be much better placed either as a prelude to the church service or at the wedding banquet. If such readings are to be a part of the service of marriage in the church, they should not replace the scriptures, nor should they be read as part of the liturgy of the word.

While it seems obvious and normal to address a wedding homily to the couple who are being married, preachers need to remember that their words are being overheard by the congregation, a congregation made up, for the most part, of men and women who are remembering their own wedding day, recalling the joys and sorrows of their own marriage, and probably wondering if the couple up front can possibly have any idea of what marriage is really like. Wedding homilies can be, for those who overhear them, an invitation to the married couples present to give thanks for the love they have found, to repent of the sorrow they have caused, and to rededicate themselves to the continual giving and taking that marriage involves. Preachers should also keep in mind that there will very likely be present in the congregation men and women who have either fallen away or been driven away from the church or who, whether "churched" or "unchurched," may never have really heard the gospel. In other words, marriages (as well as funerals) provide an occasion for evangelization in that there may well be those present who will be hearing for the first time just what the Christian faith is all about. This more pointedly kerygmatic emphasis is certainly not out of place in a wedding homily, for in the coming together of two people to pledge their love to one another in Christ, we quickly find ourselves at the heart of the Christian gospel, which affirms that "in this is love, not that we loved God but that he loved us and sent his Son to be the expiation for our sins. Beloved, if God so loved us, we also ought to love one another" (I John 4:10-11).

Finally, it is in the celebration of marriage that preachers will probably find the greatest number of opportunities to engage in an ecumenical service of worship. In such services, it is important that every effort be made to preserve the integrity of the rite of the church in which the marriage is being celebrated. The goal of the ecumenical movement, liturgically speaking, is not some kind of ritual hybrid, made up of bits and pieces of the rituals of various Christian denominations, but rather a respect for the legitimacy and authenticity of the different liturgical traditions that have been developed and passed down. Thus, if the wedding of a Lutheran woman and a Catholic man takes place in the bride's church with the Lutheran pastor presiding and a Roman Catholic priest assisting, the Lutheran ritual of marriage should be followed and the Lutheran pastor should preach. If the wedding were to take place in the Catholic church with the priest presiding and the Lutheran minister assisting, the Catholic ritual should be followed and the priest should preach. In each case, since the homily is an integral part of the liturgical rite, it should be preached by the presiding minister.

FUNERALS

While there is a certain similarity between funerals and weddings in that the congregation that gathers is made up of people who come together for this particular occasion rather than of an already formed community that gathers regularly to worship, there are significant differences that go beyond those that are obvious. The first of these is that the funeral liturgy is rarely prepared with the same kind of care and attention that goes into the wedding ceremony. It is true that there are some individuals and families who do consciously prepare for their funerals. Frequently they are involved with self-help groups for people dying of cancer or with the hospice movement for the terminally ill. Priests and ministers who are invited to participate in such planning, or who judge it opportune to initiate the idea, will find that discussing the details of the funeral will make for a liturgical celebration that is expressive of the hope and the faith of one member of the Christian community and of the community as a whole. They may also discover that such planning will establish an environment of trust and confidence that will enable the dying person to begin dealing with some personal issues that still need to be resolved.

More frequently, however, even when death is not sudden and unexpected, there is a reluctance both on the part of the person dying and of friends and family to think seriously and in detail about arrangements for the funeral. This means that what little liturgical planning there is usually takes place in the couple of days that elapse between the time of death and the time of the funeral and burial. During that period of time the family may be so occupied with other arrangements, or so indisposed by grief, that most of the details of the liturgy will have to be attended to by those who will actually be conducting the service.

It is customary in the Roman Catholic Church for the rite of Christian burial to include the celebration of the eucharist. Although the practice is not common in some other Christian churches, recent publications indicate that it is being introduced. For instance, the *Lutheran Book of Worship* notes that "when Holy Communion is celebrated, the service continues with the Peace."[1]

And the Section on Worship of the Board of Discipleship of The United Methodist Church, while admitting that "provision for the Lord's Supper at the funeral may seem strange to United Methodists," goes on to speak of its appropriateness: "Holy Communion is proclamation of the gospel message of death and resurrection par excellence with all of its overtones of penitence and faith, of brokenness and healing, of sorrow and joy. In this sense the Sacrament is as evangelical—indeed as evangelistic—an act as the church performs."[2]

When the eucharist is celebrated it is not difficult to see that the motive for praise and thanksgiving is the victory over death and the promise of resurrection that is offered us in the death and resurrection of Christ. Frequently it will also be possible to include as a motive for thanksgiving some specific references to the life of the person who has died. The introduction to the Roman Catholic rite of Christian burial specifically says that the prohibition of a eulogy is not meant to exclude "an expression of praise and gratitude to God for his gifts, particularly the gift of a Christian life, to the deceased person" (#41). Such concrete references to the person who has died can be, in the words of the Methodist publication quoted above, "a means of summarily reviewing and cherishing the life of the deceased, and then of letting go, reinforcing the finality of death even while evoking marvel before the color and individuality of human life."[3]

Given the regularity with which funeral homilies become almost a premature canonization of the deceased, however, we need frequently to remind ourselves that the reason we can give thanks at the funeral of a sister or brother in Christ is not so much because of the greatness of their works, but because of what God has done for them in Christ. Robert Hovda put it well in writing of the ease with which we resort to eulogies, especially in a funeral for a man or woman who was a leader of some kind: "If we are so little awed by the gospel and so overawed by human greatness, something is deeply wrong and our values need sharp scrutiny."[4] In those cases where custom or propriety seem to demand some kind of personal testimony, such a talk would best be given by someone who knew the person well and placed near the end of the service.

PREACHING AT OTHER LITURGICAL SERVICES

Because of the principle stated by the Second Vatican Council that "whenever rites according to their specific nature, make provision for communal celebration involving the presence and active participation of the faithful, this way of celebrating them is to be preferred, as far as possible, to a celebration that is individual and quasi-private."[5] Roman Catholics have come to see and participate in communal celebrations of the sacrament of the sick (formerly known as extreme unction) and of the sacrament of reconciliation (also referred to as penance or confession), both of which in earlier days were almost always exclusively private affairs. In such services the principle of liturgical preaching that has been enunciated throughout the book will hold: the word of God is invoked to interpret people's lives in such a way that they will be able to participate in the sacramental action with faith. Thus, in celebrations of the sacrament of the sick, preaching should enable the sick to trust in God's power to heal them if it be his will (see Luke 5:12) and even to rejoice in their sufferings by seeing them as a way of completing Christ's afflictions for the sake of his body, the church (Col. 1:24). Preaching at communal celebrations of the sacrament of reconciliation, all too often little more than an extended examination of conscience, should be directed toward enabling people to accept God's mercy and forgiveness (often harder to do than to accept punishment), to be reconciled with God and with one another, and thus to turn away from whatever it is that has been a cause of alienation.

The principle of the liturgical homily as an enabling word also holds for the many services outlined in the books of worship of other Christian churches and communities. At least to this separated brother, it would seem that the preaching of a homily or sermon in such services as those for the Installation of a Commissioned Church Worker (Presbyterian), for Corporate Confession and Forgiveness

(Lutheran), Renewal of the Covenant (Methodist), or for the Celebration of a New Ministry (Episcopal) should be to enable the people particularly involved and the congregation as a whole to enter into the service in a spirit appropriate to the rite being celebrated. We gather not simply to be onlookers but to be participants. And we are equipped for this noble task by the preaching of the good news. For it is there that we find the word that enables us to see our lives not as isolated and meaningless ciphers, but as part of the vast family of God, which is the constant recipient of God's sustaining love and which finds its strength by rejoicing in the Lord (Neh. 8:10).

NOTES

CHAPTER I: The Bible and the Liturgical Year

1. The word "liturgy" comes from the Greek *leitos* (pertaining to the people) and *ergon* (work).
2. "The homily must then be understood in its uniqueness as the form of discourse designed to bring the word of God to expression in the concrete situation of the hearers." David J. Randolph, *The Renewal of Preaching* (Philadelphia: Fortress Press, 1969), p. 19.
3. Quoted in A. Allan McArthur, *The Christian Year and Lectionary Reform* (London: SCM Press, 1958), p. 27.
4. Conrad Massa, "Preaching as Confluence," *The Princeton Seminary Bulletin*, II:2 (N.S. 1979), p. 111.
5. Jean-Jacques von Allmen, *Preaching and Congregation*, trans. B. L. Nicholas (London: Lutterworth Press, 1962), p. 27.
6. Gustav Wingren, *The Living Word*, trans. Victor C. Pogue (Philadelphia: Muhlenberg Press, 1960), p. 22.
7. J. Winston Pearce, *Planning Your Preaching* (Nashville: Broadman Press, 1967), p. 60.
8. Harry Emerson Fosdick, "What Is the Matter with Preaching?" *Harpers*, July, 1928. Reprinted in *Harry Emerson Fosdick's Art of Preaching*, ed. Lionel Crocker (Springfield, Ill.: Charles C. Thomas, 1971), p. 30.
9. Eric Warner, *The Sacred Bridge* (New York: Columbia University Press, 1959), p. 50.
10. *Ancient Near Eastern Texts*, pp. 331 ff. Quoted by Lloyd Bailey, "The Lectionary in Critical Perspective," *Interpretation* 31 (April, 1977): 140.
11. J. A. Lamb, "The Place of the Bible in the Liturgy, in *The Cambridge History of the Bible*, I (New York: Cambridge University Press, 1970), 564.
12. Warner, *The Sacred Bridge*, p. 55.
13. C. T. Ruddick, "Behold I Send My Messenger," *Journal of Biblical Literature* 88 (December, 1969): 416.
14. Adrian Nocent, *The Liturgical Year*, trans. Matthew J. O'Connell, IV (Collegeville, Minn.: The Liturgical Press, 1977), 9-14.
15. It is true that this verse from Acts presents a summary of the life of the Christian community in Jerusalem and not a description of the kind of service held on the first day of the week. However, the reference to the breaking of the bread and to Paul's discourse in the account of the gathering at Troas would lead us to believe

that these two elements of the communal life in Jerusalem were also part of the celebration of the Lord's Day.

16. Dix, *The Shape of the Liturgy*, 2nd ed. (London: A. & C. Black, 1945).
17. Justin Martyr, The First Apology, chapter 67, in *Writings of Saint Justin Martyr*, trans. Thomas B. Falls (New York: Christian Heritage, 1948), pp. 106-7. A description of the eucharistic celebration following a baptism, almost identical in structure to the regular Sunday eucharist, is found in chapter 65.
18. Translation in The Fathers of the Church, vol. 1, *The Apostolic Fathers*, trans. Francis X. Glenn *et al.* (New York: Cima Publishing Co., 1947), pp. 171-86.
19. Leonel L. Mitchell, *The Meaning of Ritual* (New York: Paulist Press, 1977), p. 70.
20. ὁ προεστὼς διὰ λόγου τὴν νουθεσίαν καὶ πρόκλησιν τῆς τῶν καλῶν τούτων μιμήσεως ποιεῖται. "The president by means of the word makes an admonition and invitation of the imitation of all these beautiful things." Apology I, chapter 67.
21. A good overview of this development, with special reference to the renewed interest in the liturgical year on the part of contemporary Protestant Churches, can be found in *Seaons of the Gospel: Resources for the Christian Year*, Supplemental Worship Resources 6 (Nashville: Abingdon, 1979), pp. 17-27.
22. Louis Bouyer, *Liturgical Piety* (Notre Dame: University of Notre Dame Press, 1955), p. 190.
23. *Ibid.* See *Egeria's Travels*, ed. John Wilkinson (London: SPCK, 1971), pp. 125, 139.
24. *Word and Table. A Basic Pattern of Sunday Worship for United Methodists* (Nashville: Abingdon, 1976), p. 60.
25. Note on John 19:14 in the New American Bible (New York: P. J. Kenedy & Sons, 1970).
26. The major portion of Edward Schillebeeckx's recent work, *Jesus. An Experiment in Christology*, trans. Hubert Hoskins (New York: Seabury Press, 1979), is devoted to a study of the historical foundations of the kerygma.
27. McArthur, *The Christian Year and Lectionary Reform*, p. 64.
28. *Ibid.*, p. 67.
29. Pearce, *Planning Your Preaching*, p. 32.

CHAPTER II: The Structure and Use of the Lectionary

1. James White, *Christian Worship in Transition* (Nashville: Abingdon, 1976), p. 139.
2. See the Appendix for a partial listing of such resources.
3. James White, "Preface," A *Lectionary* (Princeton: Consultation on Church Union, 1974), p. 1.
4. Godfrey Diekmann, "Labores coetuum a studiis: De Lectionibus in Missa," *Notitiae* 1 (November, 1975): 33-37.
5. "Prius Propheta legitur, et apostolus, et sic Evangelium." Ambrose, In Psalmum 118, 17, 10 (PL 15:1443). The tradition was also kept in the Armenian rite. Rome may have kept the practice until the fifth century and the Byzantine rite until the

seventh century. Churches in the Nestorian tradition used four readings (law, prophets, apostle, gospel), as did the Coptic Churches. Syrian Churches had six readings. See Gaston Fontaine, "Commentarium ad Ordinem Lectionum Missae," *Notitiae* 5 (1979): 262.

6. Introduction to the Roman Catholic Lectionary, VIIa.
7. Lamb, "The Place of the Bible in the Liturgy," p. 572.
8. Fontaine, "Commentarium ad Ordinem Lectionum Missae," p. 265.
9. *Ibid.*, p. 266.
10. In fidelity to an early tradition: see Augustine, Sermon 315 (PL 38:1426), and Chrysostom, Homily on the Beginning of the Acts of the Apostles 4,3 (PG 51:101).
11. White, "Preface," p. 1.
12. Nocent, *The Liturgical Year*, IV, 2.
13. Gerard Sloyan, "The Lectionary as a Context for Interpretation," *Interpretation* 31 (April, 1977): 138.
14. *Ibid.*
15. Nocent, *The Liturgical Year*, IV, 6. Emphasis added.
16. Placid V. Murray, "The People and the Book," *The Furrow* 22 (July, 1971): 396.
17. J. D. Crichton, *The Once and Future Liturgy* (Dublin: Veritas Publications, 1977), p. 59.
18. Reginald Fuller, *What Is Liturgical Preaching?* (London: SCM Press, 1957), p. 45.
19. "As Wilhelm Vischer put it, Jesus Christ provides the vowel-points which give a sense to the consonants of the Hebrew text." Von Allmen, *Preaching and Congregation*, p. 25.
20. Nocent, *The Liturgical Year*, IV, 6.
21. Some older Roman Catholic manuals of sacramental theology used to refer to this passage to indicate when Jesus "instituted" the sacrament of marriage. Thus Antonius Piolanti: *De tempore institutionis dissonant auctores. Alii dicunt in Cana Galilaeae, quando Christus sua praesentia nuptias sanctificavit. . . . De Sacramentis*, 5th ed. (Rome: Marietti, 1955), p. 489.
22. Excellent examples of such preaching are to be found in Lawrence Stookey's *Living in a New Age* (Lima, Ohio: C.S.S. Publishing Co., 1978). All the homilies in this collection flow out of the second reading in the Sundays after Easter, year B.
23. Fuller, *What Is Liturgical Preaching?* p. 25.

CHAPTER III. The Pastoral Use of the Lectionary

1. *Twenty Centuries of Great Preaching*, vol. 1, *Biblical Sermons to Savanarola*, ed. Clyde E. Fant, Jr., and William M. Pinson, Jr. (Waco: Word Books, 1971), p. v.
2. It is this understanding of the liturgical homily that Jean Danielou uses in his masterful work *The Bible and the Liturgy* (Notre Dame: University of Notre Dame Press, 1956).
3. *Ibid.*, Editor's note, p. vii.
4. Edgar Jackson, *How to Preach to People's Needs* (Grand Rapids: Baker Book House, 1970), p. 14.

5. Harold Knoll, "A Sermon on Sermons," *Vital Speeches of the Day* 45 (February 1, 1979): 248.
6. Harvey F. Egan, "Behind that sermon you hear: Analysis from an inside source," The Minneapolis *Star,* June 6, 1979.
7. (Valley Forge: Judson Press, 1977.)
8. *The Roman Missal, General Instruction and The Order of the Mass* (Collegeville, Minn.: The Liturgical Press, 1970).
9. *Lectionary for Mass* (Collegeville, Minn.: The Liturgical Press, 1970), p. xxi.
10. Jean-Jacques von Allmen, *Worship, Its Theology and Practice,* trans. Harold Knight and W. Fletcher Fleet (London: Lutterworth Press, 1965), p. 132.
11. The title of David Babin's excellent work on liturgical preaching (New York: Seabury Press, 1976).
12. Fred Craddock devotes the whole of his book *Overhearing the Gospel* (Nashville: Abingdon, 1978) to a meditation on these words.
13. Frederick Buechner, *The Magnificent Defeat* (New York: Seabury Press, 1966), p. 10.
14. Henry H. Mitchell, *The Recovery of Preaching* (San Francisco: Harper & Row, 1977), p. 41.
15. Harold Rugg, *Imagination* (New York: Harper & Bros., 1963), p. 289.
16. Francis McNutt, *How to Prepare a Sermon* (Ottawa: Novalis, n.d.), p. 11.
17. *Preaching and Congregation,* p. 47.
18. Karl Barth, *The Preaching of the Gospel,* trans. B. E. Hooke (Philadelphia: Westminster Press, 1963), p. 53.
19. See Theodore Clevenger, Jr., *Audience Analysis* (Indianapolis: Bobbs-Merrill, 1966), p. 83.
20. See Huber W. Ellingsworth and Theodore Clevenger, Jr., *Speech and Social Action* (Englewood Cliffs, N.J.: Prentice Hall, 1967), pp. 114-26.
21. Clevenger, *Audience Analysis,* p. 91.

CHAPTER IV: Preaching and Sacrament

1. Quoted by Fuller, *What Is Liturgical Preaching?* p. 16.
2. *Preaching and Congregation,* p. 41.
3. Bernard Cooke, *Ministry to Word and Sacrament* (Philadelphia: Fortress Press, 1976), p. 332.
4. *Preaching and Congregation,* p. 41.
5. Charles Davis, "The Theology of Preaching, *Clergy Review* 45 (1960): 534.
6. *Word and Table,* p. 46.
7. *Overhearing the Gospel,* p. 47.
8. John Knox, *The Integrity of Preaching* (Nashville: Abingdon Press, 1957), p. 76.
9. *The Recovery of Preaching,* p. 58.
10. Ed. James Cox (Nashville: Abingdon, 1978).
11. The Augsburg Confession, in fact, speaks of retaining "almost all the customary ceremonies" (Article XXIV).
12. Edwin O'Connor, *The Edge of Sadness* (Boston: Little, Brown, 1961), p. 18.
13. Fuller, *What Is Liturgical Preaching?* p. 12.
14. See Mitchell, *The Meaning of Ritual,* pp. 108 ff.

CHAPTER V: Preaching at the Eucharist

1. A thorough analysis of eucharistic action within this framework of gathering, proclaiming, and renewing can be found in Lucien Deiss, *God's Word and God's People* (Collegeville, Minn.: The Liturgical Press, 1976).
2. Marianne Sawicki, Editor's Note, *Liturgy* 24 (Fall, 1979): 4.
3. *Preaching and Congregation*, pp. 10-11.
4. White, *Christian Worship in Transition*, p. 87.
5. Fuller, *What Is Liturgical Preaching?* p. 12.
6. Robert Hovda, *Dry Bones: Living Worship Guides to Good Liturgy* (Washington: The Liturgical Conference, 1973), p. 61.
7. The Standing Liturgical Commission of the Protestant Episcopal Church in the United States of America, *Prayer Book Studies XVII* (New York: The Church Pension Fund, 1966), p. 27.
8. Flannery O'Connor, *The Habit of Being*, letters selected and edited by Sally Fitzgerald (New York: Farrar, Strauss & Giroux, 1979), p. 511.
9. *Ibid.* Emphasis added.
10. J. N. Crespel, "Parole et sacrement," *Verbum Caro* 21 (1967): 13.
11. In Cox, *Twentieth-Century Pulpit*, p. 64.
12. Gregory Smith, "A Worthy Book," *Liturgy* 23 (March, 1978): 22.
13. *Preaching and Congregation*, p. 57.
14. John Burke, *Gospel Power* (New York: Alba House, 1978), p. 77.
15. Donald Macleod, "The Homily and the Sermon," *Pulpit Digest*, January–February, 1975, p. 14.
16. See Wm. D. Thompson and Gordon C. Bennett, *Dialogue Preaching* (Valley Forge: Judson Press, 1969), p. 9, for a discussion of these two uses of the term "dialogic."
17. *Lectures on Preaching* (London: Macmillan, 1895), p. 38. Quoted in James Cox, *A Guide to Biblical Preaching* (Nashville: Abingdon, 1976), p. 114.
18. Eduard R. Rieger, "Preaching in the Context of the Daily Prayer of the Church," *Response* 17 (1977): 39.
19. *Preaching and Congregation*, p. 34.
20. For further reasoning in favor of lay preaching at the Eucharist, see Maureen Carroll, O.P., and Kathleen Cannon, O.P., "Enfleshing the Word: The Case for Lay Preachers," *Liturgy* 24 (May–June, 1979): 31-34.
21. *Word and Table*, p. 46.
22. See the First Apology of Justin Martyr: "Then [following the admonition of the president of the assembly] we all stand up together and offer up our prayers." Full text on p. 22.
23. For details, see Frederick R. McManus, "The Genius of the Roman Rite Revisited," *Worship* 54 (July, 1980): 372-73.
24. Fuller, *What Is Liturgical Preaching?* p. 10.
25. *Word and Table*, p. 35.
26. See Richard Toporoski, "The Language of Worship," *Worship* 52 (November, 1978): 489-508, for some enlightening and provocative comments on the characteristics of ritual language and the difficulties presented by the common texts of contemporary English liturgy.

27. The evolution of the eucharistic prayer from oral improvisation to written texts is traced by Allan Bouley in *The Anaphora: From Freedom to Formula* (Washington: Catholic University Press, 1980).

28. *Rule for Monasteries*, chapter 19.

CHAPTER VI: Preaching at Baptisms, Weddings, and Funerals

1. *Lutheran Book of Worship* (Minneapolis: Augsburg Publishing House, 1978), p. 210.

2. *A Service of Death and Resurrection*, Supplemental Worship Resources 7 (Nashville: Abingdon, 1979), p. 66.

3. *Ibid.*, p. 59.

4. Robert Hovda, *Manual of Celebration* (Washington: The Liturgical Conference, 1970), p. 21 (funerals).

5. Constitution on the Sacred Liturgy, #27.

FOR FURTHER READING

CHAPTER I: The Bible and the Liturgical Year

The Church Year, Calendar and Lectionary. Prepared by the Inter-Lutheran Commission on Worship. Minneapolis: Augusburg, 1973.

Knox, John. *The Integrity of Preaching.* Nashville: Abingdon Press, 1957.

Nocent, Adrian. *The Liturgical Year,* 4 volumes. Trans. Matthew O'Connell. Collegeville, Minn.: The Liturgical Press, 1977.

Seasons of the Gospel: Resources for the Christian Year. Supplemental Worship Resources 6. Nashville: Abingdon, 1979.

CHAPTER II: The Structure and Use of the Lectionary

Interpretation. Volume 31. The entire issue is devoted to the lectionary.

A Lectionary. Princeton: Consultation on Church Union, 1974.

McArthur, Allan. *The Christian Year and Lectionary Reform.* London: SCM Press, 1958.

CHAPTER III: The Pastoral Use of the Lectionary

Craddock, Fred B. *Overhearing the Gospel.* Nashville: Abingdon, 1978.

Crum, Milton. *Manual on Preaching.* Valley Forge, Pa.: Judson Press, 1977.

Howe, Reuel L. *Partners in Preaching.* New York: Seabury Press, 1967.

von Allmen, Jean-Jacques. *Preaching and Congregation.* Trans. B. L. Nicholas. London: Lutterworth Press, 1962.

CHAPTER IV: Preaching and Sacrament

Babin, David E. *Week In, Week Out.* New York: Seabury Press, 1976.

Fuller, Reginald. *What Is Liturgical Preaching?* London: SCM Press, 1957.

Knox, John. *The Integrity of Preaching.* Nashville: Abingdon Press, 1957.

Macleod, Donald. *Word and Sacrament.* Englewood Cliffs, N.J.: Prentice Hall, 1960.

CHAPTER V: Preaching at the Eucharist

Hovda, Robert W. *Strong, Loving and Wise.* Washington, D.C.: The Liturgical Conference, 1976.

Rahner, Karl. "The Word and the Eucharist," *Theological Investigations*. Vol. IV, pp. 253-86. Trans. Kevin Smyth. Baltimore: Helicon Press, 1966.

Word and Table: A Basic Pattern of Sunday Worship for United Methodists. Alternative Rituals Editorial Committee, United Methodist Church. Nashville: Abingdon, 1976.

APPENDIX

It is evident that homiletic aids based on a common (or near common) lectionary can be of immense help to preachers. Such resources can make available to them exegetical materials they might not otherwise have access to, can help them hear the scriptural texts for a particular day in dialogue with one another, and can alert them to the added nuances of meaning that texts can have when read at a particular season and in a particular liturgical context.

But such aids can also be a hindrance to creative and responsible preaching. This happens when the homiletic resource does the work for the preacher, rather than aiding in this work. The resource then becomes little better than the medieval homilary, which provided ready-made sermons for the priest and which was aptly titled *"Dormi Secure"*—"Sleep Tight" (you don't have a sermon to worry about).

This listing of homiletic aids based on the lectionary will therefore reflect my bias in favor of materials that help preachers dwell with the text rather than remove them from it. Although the provision of model homilies or lists of illustrative materials may benefit some preachers, I believe that in the long run this kind of assistance does more to stifle creativity than to foster it.

BOOKS

Fuller, Reginald. *Preaching the New Lectionary.* 1974. The Liturgical Press, Collegeville, MN 56321.

An exegetical study of the pericopes of the Roman Catholic lectionary by a noted Episcopal exegete. Exegesis of the responsorial psalm is included, along with suggestions for various ways of moving toward the homily.

Maertens, Thierry, and Frisque, Jean. *Guide for the Christian Assembly*. 1971–74. Nine volumes. Fides Claretian Press, Notre Dame, IN 46556.

Extensive exegetical materials and theological reflection on the texts for all the Sundays and major feasts of the Roman Catholic lectionary. Additional volumes provide exegetical commentary on the weekday readings and the readings for the sanctoral cycle.

Nocent, Adrian. *The Liturgical Year*. 1977. Four volumes. The Liturgical Press, Collegeville, MN 56321.

Especially helpful in providing historical and theological background for the feasts and seasons of the liturgical year. Exegetical commentary on the Sunday lessons is also provided.

Sloyan, Gerard. *A Commentary on the New Lectionary*. 1975. Paulist Press, 545 Island Rd., Ramsey, N.J. 07446.

An excellent example of a commentary that helps preachers do their own work rather than doing it for them. Based on the Roman Catholic lectionary.

Proclamation. Twenty-six volumes. Fortress Press, 2900 Queen Lane, Philadelphia, PA 19129.

These paperbacks offer "exegetical interpretations of the lessons for each Sunday and many of the festivals of the church year, plus homiletical ideas and insights. The basic thrust of the series is ecumenical" (from the General Preface). *Proclamation Commentaries* are also available.

SUBSCRIPTION SERVICES

Celebration—A Creative Worship Service. P.O. Box 281, Kansas City, MO 64141.

Based on the Roman Catholic lectionary. Exegetical comments are brief (about 250 words per pericope) but seem to be on target. The "Introductions to the Readings" and the "Homily," however, seem to have been prepared without reference to the exegesis provided. Other liturgically related materials are included in the service.

Good News. 1229 S. Santee St., Los Angeles, CA 90015.

Based on the Roman Catholic lectionary, but an ecumenical commentary is included for the asking at no extra cost. The exegetical comments are brief and elementary, and there is no apparent connection between the exegesis and the homily models.

Homily Service. 810 Rhode Island Ave., NE, Washington, DC 20018.

A comprehensive service that includes reference to all lectionaries (though geared to the Roman Catholic), exegesis, a "personalist and therapeutic" reflection on the texts, ideas and illustrations, a homily "in rough form," and questions to guide the discussion of an adult Bible study group.

Word and Witness: A Complete Resource for Celebration and Proclaiming the Gospel. 3003 Congress Ave., Lake Worth, FL 33461.

One of the best Protestant services, offering exegetical commentary on the COCU lectionary readings: prayers, readings, and litanies; "images and ideas"—quotations from relevant writings; and a sermon approach.

A fuller listing of available materials can be obtained from the Board of Discipleship of The United Methodist Church, P.O. Box 840, Nashville, TN 37202.

INDEX OF SUBJECTS

INDEX OF SCRIPTURE REFERENCES